The Modern Grimoire
of
Sympathetic Magic

*1000+ Charms and Modern Rituals
for Healing, Love, Prosperity,
Protection and More*

A. B. ROWAN

Copyright © 2025 by A B Rowan

All rights reserved.

No part of this book may be reproduced, stored in a retrieval system, or transmitted in any form or by any means—electronic, mechanical, photocopying, recording, or otherwise—without the prior written permission of the publisher, except for brief quotations in critical reviews or articles.

ISBN 978-1-918219-12-8

First Edition: 2025

Published by: Cosmic Jive Publishing
www.cosmicjivepublishing.com
For permissions and inquiries, contact:
info@cosmicjivepublishing.com

The views, opinions, beliefs, and practices expressed in this book are those of the author and do not necessarily reflect the views or opinions of the publisher. The publisher is not responsible for the accuracy, completeness, or effectiveness of the content within this book, nor does the publisher endorse or advocate for any specific practices, rituals, or beliefs described herein.

This book is presented as a work of cultural, historical, and personal exploration and is intended for educational and entertainment purposes only. Readers are encouraged to approach the material with an open mind and to conduct their own research and consultation before applying any of the concepts, techniques, or ideas discussed.

The publisher disclaims any liability for any actions, decisions, or outcomes that may result from the use or misuse of the information provided in this book.

Disclaimer

The information contained in this book is intended for educational, entertainment, and informational purposes only. The practices, rituals, and folk wisdom described herein are based on historical, cultural, and traditional beliefs and should not be taken as scientific fact or medical advice.

The author and publisher of this book do not guarantee the effectiveness, safety, or outcomes of any practices, spells, or remedies mentioned. Readers are encouraged to use their own judgment and discretion when applying any of the ideas or techniques presented.

Magic, spirituality, and folk wisdom are deeply personal and subjective experiences. What works for one individual may not work for another. Always respect cultural traditions and practices, and avoid appropriating or misusing them.

This book is not a substitute for professional guidance, whether medical, psychological, legal, or spiritual. If you are experiencing physical or mental health issues, please consult a qualified professional.

By engaging with this book, you acknowledge that the author and publisher are not responsible for any actions, decisions, or consequences that may arise from the use of its contents. Practice all forms of magic and folk wisdom responsibly, ethically, and with respect for yourself and others.

Thank you for reading, and may your journey be filled with wisdom and wonder.

About the Author

A.B. Rowan is a writer and practitioner of modern folk magic, weaving tradition with practicality to create accessible and meaningful guides for the contemporary seeker. With a lifelong passion for symbols, stories, and the subtle connections that thread through everyday life, Rowan's work demystifies ancient practices, making them relevant and approachable for today's world.

Rooted in the belief that magic is not reserved for the few but is a birthright for all, Rowan emphasizes simplicity and intention. In their writing, everyday objects—a candle, a coin, or a piece of thread—are revealed as potent tools for transformation, healing, and connection. By bridging the gap between old-world wisdom and modern living, Rowan empowers readers to infuse their daily lives with purpose and enchantment.

When not immersed in writing, Rowan can be found wandering through forests, nurturing a small garden, or jotting down reflections on the quiet, overlooked magic that resides in the ordinary. Their work is an invitation to see the world anew, where the mundane becomes sacred and every act holds the potential for wonder.

Preface

Magic is not locked away in dusty tomes or obscure rituals of centuries past—it thrives in the ordinary objects around you. A coffee cup, a coin, a shoelace, a sticky note: each carries symbolic power if you learn to see it. Sympathetic magic, the art of using resemblance and connection to influence the world, is one of the oldest practices known to humankind. It is also one of the most adaptable, and that makes it uniquely suited for our modern lives.

This book is a bridge. It gathers folk practices that once relied on walnuts, toads, and herbs grown in cottage gardens and translates them into the everyday world of city apartments, office desks, and smartphones. You will not need a witch's chest of rare items. Instead, you'll learn to craft charms from sugar packets, glass jars, keys, coins, and even emojis. The point is not the rarity of the object but the meaning we weave into it. Magic lives in symbol, and symbols live everywhere.

This guide aims to give you more than a collection of charms: it offers principles, methods, and exercises to help you see your life as enchanted, to craft your own magic, and to live more intentionally.

Introduction
Entering the Language of Magic

Everywhere you go, magic waits in plain sight. You might not call it that, not at first, but you already live inside its language. Think about it. You blow out birthday candles and make a secret wish. You slip a lucky coin into your pocket before a big test. You hesitate to walk under a ladder, or you find yourself knocking on wood, "just in case." You've traced your fingers over an old photograph, swearing you could almost feel the person there.

These aren't accidents. They aren't quirks of culture that somehow slipped past logic. They are fragments of something much older, much deeper — a way of seeing the world through connections, resemblances, and symbols. This way of seeing is called sympathetic magic.

Sympathetic magic is one of the simplest, most universal forms of human magic. Its rules are easy to grasp: *like affects like* and *once connected, always connected*. In other words, resemblance creates influence, and contact creates bond. If you want to attract love, you use something that symbolizes love. If you want to release sorrow, you give it to the fire, the river, or the wind — because that element will carry it away.

You already know this instinctively. That's why you might feel relief tearing up a letter from someone who hurt you, or why writing a goal on paper and pinning it above your desk feels like setting the course. You've practiced sympathetic magic without ever calling it by name.

The Secret You Already Know

The beauty of sympathetic magic is that it doesn't require belief in complicated doctrines. It only asks you to admit something you've always felt: that the world is woven together by unseen threads, and that symbols can tug at those threads.

- You kiss a photograph of someone far away. Why? Because part of you believes the kiss travels along that image to the person themselves.

- You clutch a piece of jewelry handed down through your family. Why? Because it still hums with the presence of those who touched it before.

- You tie a ribbon around your finger to remind yourself of something. Why? Because the ribbon becomes memory incarnate.

These are everyday acts of magic. Quiet, unnoticed, but powerful.

Why Now?

We live in an age of glowing screens, online orders, and endless information. And yet, more and more people are drawn back to charms, rituals, candles, herbs, and folk practices. Why?

Because sympathetic magic gives us something our modern world rarely does: a way to touch our intentions, to hold them in our hands.

When life feels overwhelming, a simple act like lighting a candle or tying a knot brings your focus back. When the future feels uncertain, writing a wish on paper and folding it carefully makes that wish real in the moment. When grief weighs heavy, dropping a stone into a river gives the sorrow a physical place to go.

We don't turn to magic because we believe it will solve everything instantly. We turn to it because it restores agency. It says: *Here is something I can do, right now, to shape my world.*

The Two Laws: Like and Contact

Let's break down the two "laws" of sympathetic magic in plain words.

Law One: Like Affects Like

If something looks like or represents what you want, it can influence it. Walnuts for warts. Red roses for love. Coins for prosperity. This is why we use symbols — they bridge the gap between desire and reality.

Law Two: Once Connected, Always Connected

Things that were once linked remain linked. Hair, nails, clothing, photographs — all hold a charge of connection. That's why you might still feel something stirring in you when you hold a letter from someone you haven't seen in years.

Put these two together, and you have the entire skeleton of sympathetic magic. With them, you can build thousands of charms.

Everyday Magic Is Everywhere

When people imagine "magic," they often picture dark cloaks, old grimoires, strange powders, or animal parts preserved in jars. But the real magic is far simpler, and far closer.

- A pinch of salt on the windowsill.
- A coin placed carefully in your shoe.
- A ribbon tied around a jar.
- A candle lit with a whispered name.
- A loaf of bread shared between friends.

These are tools as humble as they are powerful. You can find them in your kitchen, your pocket, your desk drawer. What matters is not exotic rarity but symbolic resonance. A Story of the Wart and the Walnut

Let me tell you a story. A woman brings her child to a village healer. The child's hand is covered with warts, and nothing has worked. The healer takes a walnut, rubs it across each blemish, and then buries it deep in the ground. "As the walnut rots," the healer says, "so will the warts vanish."

Within weeks, the child's hand clears. Was it the walnut's chemical nature? Maybe. Was it the act of rubbing and focusing the intention? Surely. But at its heart, it was sympathetic logic: the walnut resembled the wart, and by transferring it symbolically, healing could begin.

This is the magic you are about to learn — the power of metaphor turned into practice.

What This Book Will Teach You

This book is not about collecting rare items or memorizing endless correspondences. It is about training your eyes to see symbols everywhere. A key is never just a key. A thread is never just a thread. A candle is never just wax and wick.

You will learn:

- How to understand the language of symbols.
- How to use everyday objects as magical tools.
- How to craft charms for healing, love, prosperity, and protection.
- How to substitute modern items for older folk practices.
- How to build your own personal grimoire of sympathetic acts.

By the time you finish, you will be able to look around your home and see dozens of ready charms waiting to be shaped.

Your First Simple Charms

Before we go any further, let me give you two easy practices to try right now.

Charm One: The Worry Stone

Find a small pebble, smooth and comforting to the touch. Hold it in your hand. Breathe your worries into it, imagining them soaking into the stone. Then set the stone outside your door, saying, "You stay here. I go free."

Charm Two: The Candle Wish

Take a birthday candle — the kind you can buy cheaply anywhere. Place it in a holder or a dish. Whisper your wish into the flame as you light it. Let the candle burn all the way down. Imagine your wish rising with the smoke.

These are not complicated. They don't need to be. They are powerful because they embody symbol, intention, and action in one.

Magic as Relationship

Sympathetic magic is not about forcing the universe to obey your will. It is about entering into relationship with it. When you use salt to cleanse, you are acknowledging salt's nature as a preserver. When you use bread to bless, you are honoring bread as the symbol of life and nourishment. When you tie a ribbon around your wrist, you are weaving yourself into the fabric of intention.

This is not superstition. This is communication. It is learning to speak back to the world in the language it already speaks to you.

An Invitation

So here is my invitation to you: step into this language. Allow yourself to see the walnut as a wart, the coin as prosperity, the candle as a star. Play with these correspondences. Experiment. Write down what works. Trust your instincts.

You are already a magician. Every time you blew out a candle or carried a lucky charm, you practiced the art. This book will simply help you remember, refine, and reclaim it.

When you are ready, turn the page. The symbols are waiting. The threads are there to be woven. The language of sympathetic magic is older than words, and it is calling you home.

Chapter One
What Is Sympathetic Magic?

Magic, at its heart, is the art of relationship. It is not about summoning lightning bolts or commanding forces beyond nature. It is about listening to the subtle echoes between things, recognizing how one form reflects another, and learning to speak that language in action. Sympathetic magic is one of the oldest expressions of this art. It is the recognition that things can influence each other because of their resemblance or their connection, even if they are not physically in contact.

The term "sympathetic magic" was made famous by Sir James Frazer in his monumental work *The Golden Bough* (first published in 1890). Frazer divided sympathetic magic into two great principles: **the Law of Similarity** (like affects like) and **the Law of Contagion** (things once in contact remain connected). While his tone was that of a Victorian scholar who often saw magic as primitive superstition, the framework he offered remains useful for understanding how folk magicians, cunning folk, healers, and witches have worked across centuries.

But to treat sympathetic magic as a relic of anthropology misses the point. We all use sympathetic magic, whether we call it that or not. We blow out birthday candles and believe our wish is carried into the flame. We wear the jersey of our favorite athlete, as though their success can rub off on us. We keep photographs of loved ones to feel closer to them, believing that an image — a likeness — is linked to the original. These are not quaint old customs; they are living proof that the human imagination still speaks the language of sympathetic resonance.

THE LAW OF SIMILARITY: LIKE AFFECTS LIKE

The first principle of sympathetic magic is that *like produces like*. To harm or heal a person, you use something that resembles them or their condition. To bring about a desired effect, you act it out in miniature. This is why a walnut — wrinkled, round, flesh encased in shell — was used in folk healing to treat warts. The logic is simple: the walnut looks like a wart, therefore the act of rubbing it across the skin draws the wart into the nut, which can then be discarded.

Across cultures, this principle shows up in countless ways:

Healing through similarity:

Ancient healers often prescribed herbs based on their resemblance to body parts. The "Doctrine of Signatures" suggested that walnuts are good for the brain because their inner kernel resembles the folds of gray matter. Kidney beans were thought to aid the kidneys. Carrots sliced across reveal a pattern like the human iris, and so were eaten for eye health.

- **Magic through imitation:**

To bring rain, people would sprinkle water on the ground, mimic the sound of thunder on drums, or pour out bowls of water as if the sky itself were being emptied. To encourage fertility, couples might sleep on freshly sown fields, imitating the union of seed and soil.

- **Protection through resemblance:**

A scarecrow is a perfect example. By resembling a human form, it stands in for the farmer, guarding crops and scaring away intruders. Dolls, figures, or effigies have been used for centuries both to protect and to curse, depending on the intention of the maker.

The power lies not in the walnut, the bean, or the drum alone, but in the recognition of a symbolic parallel — and the belief that this parallel allows energy, intention, or essence to flow.

THE LAW OF CONTAGION:
ONCE CONNECTED, ALWAYS CONNECTED

The second principle is the law of contagion: things that have once been in contact continue to influence each other, even after separation. This principle explains the use of hair, nail clippings, or personal clothing in spells. A piece of someone remains linked to the whole, and therefore can be used to affect them from a distance.

Examples include:

- **Personal links in healing or harm:**

  A lock of hair, a shred of cloth, or the impression of a footprint in earth can all serve as magical links. The cunning folk of Europe often treated illness by using a person's urine, believing it carried the essence of the sickness — and therefore could be magically cleansed or destroyed.

- **Objects with enduring connection:**

  Wedding rings hold not only the symbol of union but the physical link of having touched the skin daily. Heirlooms, family Bibles, or even a child's toy carry a lingering charge of contact with their owners.

- **Food and offerings:**

  To share bread or salt with someone is to be bound in fellowship with them. The act of eating together creates a sympathetic bond that lingers long after the meal.

In modern life, we instinctively recognize contagion magic in the way we handle mementos. A love letter still vibrates with intimacy. A photograph of the dead feels charged with presence. To burn a letter is to symbolically burn the relationship itself.

Sympathetic Magic Across Cultures

Sympathetic practices are not limited to any one tradition. They arise wherever humans notice patterns and resonances.

- **Ancient Egypt:**
  Statues of enemies were inscribed with curses and smashed, symbolically destroying the real enemy. Conversely, amulets shaped like protective gods were worn to attract the same protection.

- **Indigenous Traditions:**
  Rain dances, fertility rites, and hunting magic often use mimicry — dancing like animals, drawing their images, or reenacting successful hunts to ensure real ones.

- **European Folk Magic:**
  Knots tied in cords could bind illness, calm storms, or trap witches. Shoes hidden in chimneys were believed to catch evil spirits because shoes carried the imprint of the wearer.

- **African Diasporic Practices:**
  In hoodoo, mojo bags often include personal concerns (hair, nails, scraps of clothing) alongside symbolic items like coins or roots, uniting contagion and similarity in one portable charm.

- **Asian Traditions:**
  In Chinese folk magic, paper effigies of houses, money, or servants are burned for the dead, under the logic

that like attracts like: the burnt paper transforms into the desired object in the afterlife.

These examples remind us that sympathetic magic is not a quirky corner of European witchcraft. It is a universal mode of thinking and acting — one crossing geography and time.

Everyday Sympathetic Magic Today

While the examples above may feel exotic, sympathetic magic is alive and well in the twenty-first century.

- We hang photos of loved ones to keep them close.
- We wear clothing or jewelry associated with success.
- We avoid breaking mirrors for fear of bad luck, or toss salt over our shoulders to undo negativity.
- Athletes perform rituals like tapping shoes, kissing lucky charms, or refusing to wash jerseys after a win — direct descendants of sympathetic reasoning.
- We give flowers for love, coins for prosperity, or birthday candles for wishes.

In each case, the symbolism speaks louder than logic. We don't need scientific proof that blowing out candles brings dreams true; we need the act itself, the moment where intention, symbol, and imagination align. That is the essence of sympathetic magic.

Why Sympathetic Magic Works

Critics dismiss sympathetic magic as superstition. Yet to call it mere coincidence misses its psychological, cultural, and even spiritual potency.

Here are a few ways to understand why it continues to resonate:

Psychological focus:

Rituals give form to desire. When you rub a walnut on a wart, you are embodying the wish for removal. This focuses the mind, and the mind's focus can affect behavior, stress, and even healing outcomes.

Symbolic resonance:

Humans are symbolic creatures. Symbols speak to our subconscious, bypassing rational doubt. To burn a letter feels like closure because we've enacted the symbol of release.

Community validation:

Many charms are social. To give bread, share salt, or light candles together creates bonds, affirming belief through collective action.

Spiritual worldview:

For those who see the world as interconnected, sympathetic magic is not a trick but a recognition of invisible threads — energy, spirit, or resonance that links all things.

The Walnut and the Wart: A Story

To make this concrete, imagine a rural healer centuries ago. A mother brings her child, embarrassed by the cluster of warts on his hand. The healer reaches for a walnut, smooths its ridged surface across each blemish, then buries the nut in the earth.

By sympathetic logic, as the walnut decays, so will the warts vanish. For the child, the ritual feels real: the wart was taken into the nut, and the burial marks its departure. For the mother, the act offers hope where medicine is scarce. For the healer, the practice is both tradition and service.

Whether or not the walnut holds chemical power is irrelevant. What matters is that everyone involved believed, and through that belief, change was made possible.

Sympathetic Magic as a Living Language

Think of sympathetic magic not as a fossilized superstition but as a language — one older than writing, spoken through gesture and symbol. In this language, a walnut can mean a wart, a candle can mean the sun, a knot can mean a bond. To practice sympathetic magic is to become fluent in this symbolic grammar, able to read the world's signs and reply with gestures of your own.

As we move through this book, we will explore that grammar in depth: the vocabulary of symbols, the common tools, and the countless charms that grow from them. By the end, you will see how a handful of salt, a thread of red string, or the flicker of a flame can become potent allies.

Sympathetic magic is not about wielding exotic powers. It is about paying attention — seeing in the walnut a mirror of the wart, in the coin a promise of prosperity, in the ribbon a knot of love. It is about answering the world with symbols, and trusting that symbols carry weight.

And if you doubt it, consider this: the fact that you are reading this book at all — drawn by its title, its promise, its symbolism — is already proof that sympathetic magic works. A word led you here. A sign called you closer. That is the oldest magic of all.

Chapter Two
The Language of Symbols

If sympathetic magic is the art of making connections, then symbols are its alphabet. Every culture, every tradition, every household has relied on a symbolic grammar — a way of saying through objects and gestures what cannot always be spoken directly. To work magic, you must learn this symbolic language: how colors, shapes, numbers, and everyday items resonate, how they "stand in" for greater forces, and how to combine them in charms and rituals.

But unlike Latin or French, the language of symbols has no dictionary carved in stone. It shifts, adapts, and evolves with people. It is both universal and personal. Fire may symbolize transformation in every corner of the world, but the way you personally respond to the flicker of a candle — the memory it awakens, the emotion it stirs — gives it a private layer of meaning. In sympathetic magic, both matter.

Why Symbols Matter

Humans are symbolic thinkers by nature. A wedding ring is not just a piece of metal; it stands for a union, a promise, an entire relationship. A national flag is not just cloth; it embodies identity, history, and pride. In the same way, a candle flame can represent the sun, a red thread can represent blood, a key can represent access or opportunity.

When we use objects in sympathetic magic, we are not pretending. We are engaging in the oldest form of communication our minds know: the metaphor made tangible. This is why the charm works. It is not the object itself, but the resonance between object, meaning, and intention that creates the channel.

Universal Patterns in Symbols

Though symbols adapt, some patterns appear again and again across cultures:

Upward = Divine / Higher
Smoke rising, trees reaching skyward, birds in flight — all connect us to realms above. Raising your hands or lifting an offering mirrors this.

Downward = Root / Underworld
Burials, seeds in soil, caves and deep water — the downward direction carries meaning of endings, beginnings, hidden things.

Circle = Wholeness
The sun, the moon, the wheel — all echo completion, eternity, the cycle.

Crossroads = Choice and Power
Meeting places of roads are liminal zones, neither one path nor another, always rich in symbolic power.

Recognizing these patterns allows us to "read" the symbolic field and to consciously choose elements for our spells and charms.

The Language of Color

Color is one of the simplest and most immediate symbolic tools. Every color speaks. Here are common correspondences (not fixed laws, but guides):

Red: Passion, love, vitality, courage, danger, blood. Use red thread for binding, red candles for love, red stones for courage.

Blue: Healing, calm, truth, spirituality, protection. Blue ribbons to soothe arguments, blue candles for peace, blue water bottles for healing.

Green: Growth, money, fertility, luck, renewal. Green leaves for prosperity charms, green candles for wealth, green thread for success in studies.

Yellow/Gold: Joy, intelligence, confidence, communication, sun energy. Yellow flowers for friendship, golden coins for prosperity, yellow thread for eloquence.

Black: Absorption, banishment, protection, mystery, endings. Black stones to absorb negativity, black cloths for shielding, black candles to end harmful ties.

White: Purity, clarity, new beginnings, peace. White thread to cleanse, white candles for new ventures, white paper for wishes.

Purple: Wisdom, spiritual authority, psychic power. Purple candles for divination, purple ribbon for confidence, amethyst stones for intuition.

Practical Charm Example (Colors):

To calm a heated household, tie a blue ribbon around the leg of the kitchen table, speaking peace into the knot. The blue draws calm into the heart of the home, where meals and conversations happen.

THE LANGUAGE OF SHAPES

Shapes carry meaning in sympathetic logic:

Circle: Completeness, eternity, cycles. A ring of salt to protect, a circle drawn to define sacred space.

Triangle: Change, balance of three forces, manifestation. Triangular folds in paper charms to bring growth.

Square: Stability, structure, the four directions. Square stones or tiles for grounding rituals.

Spiral: Growth, journey inward or outward, evolution. Drawing spirals on paper for healing that unfolds over time.

Cross or X: Intersection, decision, sacred meeting place, sometimes banishment. Crossing two sticks to seal a spell.

Practical Charm Example (Shapes):

For stability in a new home, place four coins at the four corners of the property. Their square arrangement grounds and anchors the household.

THE LANGUAGE OF NUMBERS

Numbers hold power in nearly every magical system. Their symbolism can be used in repetitions (saying a charm three times), in grouping items, or in timing spells.

One: Unity, beginning, individuality.

Two: Balance, partnership, duality.

Three: Creation, completeness, movement.

Four: Stability, the material world, the elements.

Five: Humanity, change, the senses.

Seven: Mystery, spirit, luck.

Nine: Fulfillment, culmination, endings.

Practical Charm Example (Numbers):
To encourage new beginnings, write a wish on paper and fold it **once**. Place it beneath a candle, burn the candle completely, then bury the folded paper. The single fold aligns with unity and new start.

THE LANGUAGE OF PLANTS AND HERBS

Plants are some of the most available and potent symbols in magic. Each carries folklore and resonance. A few examples:

Rose: Love, attraction, beauty. Petals in bathwater for romance.

Basil: Prosperity, protection, love. Basil leaves in wallets for money.

Rosemary: Memory, cleansing, protection. Bundles burned like incense to clear spaces.

Mint: Freshness, communication, luck. Mint leaves in pockets for good fortune.

Lavender: Peace, sleep, harmony. Sachets under pillows for calm dreams.

Practical Charm Example (Herbs):
For peaceful rest, sew a small pillow filled with lavender and chamomile. Each night, as you rest your head, you enter sleep through a field of calm.

THE LANGUAGE OF ANIMALS

Animals, too, are symbols — though modern sympathetic magic often avoids harm, focusing instead on representation.

Cat: Mystery, independence, guardianship. Images of cats at doorways for protection.

Dog: Loyalty, friendship, devotion. Small dog figurines in charms for fidelity.

Birds: Freedom, spirit, messages. Feathers collected ethically for communication spells.

Bees: Community, hard work, sweetness. Honey in spells for attraction or peace.

Deer: Gentleness, renewal, vulnerability. Antler-shaped charms for growth.

Practical Charm Example (Animals):
To strengthen friendship, gift a friend a honey-sweetened pastry, symbolizing bee-lore. The act binds sweetness into the bond.

THE LANGUAGE OF HOUSEHOLD OBJECTS

The beauty of sympathetic magic lies in its practicality. Everyday objects are saturated with meaning:

Keys: Access, opportunity, unlocking. Carry an old key in a charm bag for new job prospects.

Coins: Wealth, value, exchange. Place coins in the corners of a purse to draw abundance.

Mirrors: Reflection, truth, reversal. Place a mirror facing outward at a window to deflect negativity.

- **Thread/Ribbon:** Connection, binding, continuity. Tie knots for goals, wear colored threads for intention.

- **Bread/Salt:** Hospitality, life, preservation. A loaf of bread and salt at the door blesses a home.

Practical Charm Example (Household):
To "unlock" inspiration, write your goal on paper, fold it, and place it beneath an old key on your desk. Each time you touch the key, visualize the door opening.

MAKING SYMBOLS YOUR OWN

It is important to remember that symbols are alive. They gain power not only through tradition but through personal connection. If you associate the smell of coffee with comfort and energy, then coffee beans can serve as your personal symbol of vitality. If daisies remind you of a lost loved one, they may carry special resonance in your work.

The goal is not to memorize endless lists but to develop your own **symbolic vocabulary** — one that draws on tradition while honoring your unique life.

Symbolic Substitution for the Modern World

Not everyone has access to rare herbs or exotic curios. But sympathetic magic adapts. Here are some modern substitutions that work beautifully:

- Instead of rare resins → use incense sticks from the corner store.
- Instead of exotic feathers → use paper cutouts of birds.
- Instead of toads or animal parts (used in old folk magic) → use figurines, images, or symbolic substitutes (e.g., a frog charm, toy, or sticker).
- Instead of silver coins (hard to find) → use any coin, marked with your intention.
- Instead of blood → use red ink or thread, symbolizing life essence without harm.

What matters is the connection in your mind and spirit. The symbol must speak to you — that is its true power.

A MODERN SYMBOLIC SPELL

To tie this together, here is an example spell entirely built from symbolic language:

A Charm for Confidence

- Take a small piece of yellow paper (yellow = confidence).
- Write your name three times (three = creation and completeness).
- Fold the paper into a triangle (triangle = manifestation).
- Place the folded paper under a clear glass of water (water = clarity).
- Each morning, before leaving the house, drink a sip from the glass and visualize confidence filling you.

This is sympathetic magic in its purest form: the language of color, number, shape, and element combined into an act of intention.

Conclusion: Learning to Speak Symbolically

The language of symbols is not foreign to us. It is the first language we learn as children, when we pretend a stick is a sword or a doll is a baby. It is the language of dreams, poetry, and art. To work sympathetic magic is simply to become fluent in that language once again — to see the walnut as a brain, the candle as the sun, the ribbon as a bond.

As you explore this book, begin keeping your own symbolic journal. Write down what colors, shapes, objects, and animals mean to you. Collect images, draw sketches, note the feelings they stir. Over time, you will assemble a dictionary more powerful than any borrowed list, because it will be yours.

This is the language the universe speaks in whispers. With practice, you will learn not only to listen but to reply.

Chapter Three
Tools of Everyday Magic

Magic does not require exotic ingredients or rare curios. You do not need to scour the wilderness for wolf bones, or pay fortunes for powdered gemstones. The real toolkit of the sympathetic magician is all around you: the kitchen shelf, the junk drawer, the pockets of your coat. Everyday items are already saturated with meaning. When you learn to see them through symbolic eyes, you discover that your home is a treasury of magical tools.

This chapter is not about buying more things. It is about reclaiming what you already have. Salt, thread, coins, mirrors, bread — each carries centuries of folklore and layers of symbolic resonance. With them you can heal, protect, attract, release, and bless. The trick is learning to use them with imagination and intention.

SALT: THE PRESERVER AND PROTECTOR

Salt has been sacred since the beginning of civilization. It preserves food, it cleanses, it flavors, and it purifies. In folklore, salt drives away evil, neutralizes curses, and seals boundaries. To "salt the earth" can mean to destroy, but to sprinkle salt on a threshold is to guard.

Uses:
- Sprinkle salt across doorways and windowsills for protection.
- Dissolve salt in water to make cleansing washes.
- Place a pinch of salt in a charm bag to "ground" the other ingredients.

Charms with Salt:

1. **Banishing Bad Energy:**
   Add a tablespoon of salt to a bowl of water. Stir clockwise, saying, "All that harms dissolves away." Use the water to wash your hands or sprinkle around a room.

2. **Prosperity Salt:**
   Mix salt with dried basil and keep in a small jar. Shake it when you need to draw money, visualizing abundance flowing like grains.

3. **Love Protection:**
   If a relationship feels troubled, circle a shared photograph with a ring of salt, saying, "Bound by love, shielded from harm."

WATER: THE UNIVERSAL SOLVENT

Water flows, cleanses, nourishes, and remembers. It carries immense symbolic weight in every culture: baptismal waters, sacred springs, holy wells, rain for fertility. In sympathetic magic, water is life itself.

Uses:

- Collect rainwater for renewal spells.
- Use river water for movement and change.
- Add drops of water to ink or paint to infuse intention.

Charms with Water:

1. **Healing Wash:**
   Write the illness or worry on paper. Dissolve the paper in a bowl of water, then pour the water away at a crossroads.

2. **Dream Water:**
   Before bed, place a glass of water by your bedside. Whisper your question or desire into it. In the morning, pour the water onto the ground, giving your request to the earth.

3. **Friendship Ritual:**
   Share a drink of water poured from the same jug with someone you wish to bond with. The shared liquid symbolizes shared essence.

FIRE AND FLAME

Fire transforms. It consumes, cleanses, and illuminates. Candles are one of the most widely used magical tools because their flame is a miniature sun, a symbol of life-force and will.

Uses:

- Burn candles of specific colors to set intentions.
- Use flame to destroy written worries.
- Fire is often used in sympathetic acts of transformation.

Charms with Fire:

1. **Wish Candle:**
   Write your wish on paper. Place it under a small candle of appropriate color (green for money, pink for love, blue for healing). Burn the candle completely.

2. **Breaking a Bond:**
   Write the name of a harmful influence. Pass the paper quickly through flame, then drop it into a bowl of water. Fire destroys, water neutralizes.

3. **Igniting Courage:**
   Light a red candle before a difficult task. As it burns, imagine the flame entering your chest, igniting bravery.

THREAD, STRING, AND RIBBON

A thread is never just a thread. It is connection, continuity, weaving, destiny. Knots bind; loose ends unravel. Folk magic has long used cords to tie intentions, seal promises, or create bonds.

Uses:

- Red thread for protection or vitality.
- White string for purity or beginnings.
- Black cord for banishment or endings.

Charms with Thread:

1. **Knot of Protection:**
   Tie three knots in a string while chanting protection. Wear it around the wrist until it falls away naturally.

2. **Love Binding (Gentle):**
   Tie two ribbons (one for each person) together loosely, speaking of harmony and closeness. Place them under a candle for an evening.

3. **Goal Knotting:**
   For each step toward a goal, tie a knot in a cord. Carry the cord as a record of progress.

COINS AND CURRENCY

Coins are tangible wealth: round, metal, enduring. They symbolize not just money, but exchange, value, and opportunity.

Uses:

- Place coins in shoes to "walk toward wealth."
- Bury coins in the garden to "seed" prosperity.
- Gift coins to others as blessings of luck.

Charms with Coins:

1. **Prosperity Pocket:**
   Carry three coins tied in green cloth to draw money.

2. **Opportunity Key:**
   Tape a coin to a key. Carry them together to "unlock" financial or career doors.

3. **Luck Offering:**
   Toss a coin into running water with a wish. The coin travels onward, carrying your intent.

Mirrors

Mirrors reflect, reveal, and reverse. They are liminal objects, showing both reality and illusion. In sympathetic magic, they can turn back curses, expose truth, or double power.

Uses:

- Place mirrors facing outward to repel negativity.
- Use mirrors in divination.
- Place two mirrors facing each other to magnify intent.

Charms with Mirrors:

1. **Shielding Window:**
   Hang a small mirror by a window facing out. Any ill-will sent toward the home bounces back.

2. **Truth Charm:**
   Place a mirror under a pillow when you feel someone is deceiving you. Dreams may reveal the truth.

3. **Prosperity Reflection:**
   Place a coin on a mirror during a waxing moon. As the coin doubles in reflection, imagine your wealth increasing.

BREAD AND FOOD

Bread is life. It is nourishment, community, daily sustenance. Salt and bread together are ancient emblems of hospitality. Food in magic is both offering and symbol: to eat is to take intention into the body.

Uses:

- Bake intentions into bread by speaking charms as you knead.
- Share food to seal bonds.
- Offer food to spirits or ancestors.

Charms with Bread:

1. **Blessed Loaf:**
   Bake bread with herbs like rosemary or basil. Share slices with family to bring unity.

2. **Wealth Bread:**
   Press a clean coin into dough before baking. Whoever receives the slice with the coin is blessed with prosperity.

3. **Bread Blessing**
   Bake bread, carving a symbol of health on top. Eating it internalizes healing.

STONES AND PEBBLES

Not all stones need to be crystals. Simple pebbles carry grounding power. Stones are durable, heavy, enduring. They symbolize strength, stability, and permanence.

Uses:

- Place stones at property corners for protection.
- Carry a pebble in the pocket as a worry stone.
- Use stones as markers in spellwork.

Charms with Stones:

1. **Peace Pebble:**
   Hold a smooth stone while focusing on calm. Carry it in the pocket; touch it during stressful times.

2. **Guardian Stones:**
   Place four stones around a bed for protection during sleep.

3. **Goal Marker:**
   Write a goal on a small stone with chalk. Place it somewhere visible until accomplished, then return it to nature.

PAPER AND INK

Paper is a blank slate, ink a tool of transformation. To write is to bind thought into form. In sympathetic magic, written charms, folded petitions, or drawn sigils are potent.

Uses:

- Write wishes or worries and burn, bury, or carry them.

- Fold paper into symbolic shapes.
- Draw symbols, runes, or personal marks.

Charms with Paper:

1. **Written Wish:**
   Write a desire, fold paper toward you, and place under a candle. Burn when fulfilled.

2. **Release Note:**
   Write a burden, tear into strips, scatter to the wind.

3. **Symbol Carry:**
   Draw a protective symbol on paper and tuck into a shoe or pocket.

EVERYDAY TOOLS IN COMBINATION

Most powerful of all is combining these simple tools. Salt plus water makes cleansing. Ribbon plus coin makes wealth bound to you. Bread plus herbs makes nourishment infused with charm. The beauty is not in exotic difficulty but in meaningful pairing.

The Modern Toolkit

Your magical toolkit may include:

- Salt, water, candles, thread, coins, mirrors, bread, stones, paper.
- Herbs from your spice rack.
- Household keys, buttons, ribbons, old jewelry.
- Images printed from the internet.
- Personal items charged with memory.

Everything is symbolic. Everything can speak. The magician's skill is learning to hear and reply.

Closing Thoughts

To work sympathetic magic, you do not need rare artifacts. You need eyes that see the walnut as a wart, the ribbon as a bond, the coin as prosperity. The world is full of tools waiting to be noticed.

When you walk through your home, begin asking: *What does this object symbolize? What story does it tell? How can I use it as a bridge between desire and reality?* In these questions lies the beginning of every charm.

Chapter Four
Love, Attraction, and Relationships

Love is the great magnet that has always drawn humanity to magic. From the earliest charms scratched into clay tablets to the folded paper notes hidden under pillows, sympathetic magic has been a tool for attracting, sustaining, and sweetening love. But love magic is not only about drawing a partner. It can be about cultivating self-love, strengthening friendships, maintaining harmony in marriage, or even learning how to gracefully release relationships that no longer serve you.

Old folk practices often relied on ingredients we no longer find easily—rosewater distilled in village stills, beeswax candles traded in markets, or ribbons blessed at holy shrines. But the *principle* is what matters, not the artifact. We can adapt these workings into modern life, using tea bags, sugar packets, red pens, and even phone apps as our magical tools.

Below are dozens of charms, categorized by purpose, each with variations and notes for personalization.

DRAWING NEW LOVE

1. The Apple Star Charm

Cut an apple crosswise and you will see a hidden five-pointed star inside. In many traditions, this is the star of Venus, the planet of love. Eat one half of the apple while focusing on drawing love into your life. Bury the other half outdoors to "plant" the seed of new romance.

- *Variation:* If you live in a city and cannot bury the apple, place the second half in a plant pot.

2. Sugar Packet Pillow Sweetener

Take a sugar packet from a café. Write your initials and the qualities you desire in a partner on the packet. Place it under your pillow for seven nights, asking that sweet dreams bring sweet encounters.

- *Modern twist:* If you don't want sugar under your pillow, tape it inside a notebook you journal in daily.

3. The Shoelace Knot Spell

Choose pink or red shoelaces. As you tie each knot, speak aloud qualities you desire in a partner ("kindness," "loyalty," "passion"). Wear the shoes regularly, symbolically walking toward love.

4. Perfume Mist of Attraction

Spray your perfume or cologne into the air. Step through the mist and say aloud: *"I carry the fragrance of love with me."* Perfume lingers, and so too does your intention.

- *Variation:* Use essential oil blends dabbed behind the ears.

5. Rose Tea Invitation

Brew rose tea. Drink half, and pour the other half into the soil of a plant. Say: *"As the rose blooms, so does love find me."*

Sweetening Existing Relationships

6. Cinnamon Stick Harmony

Wrap a cinnamon stick in red thread and keep it in your wallet. Cinnamon heats passion and red binds harmony.

- *Variation:* Tape it behind a framed photo of you and your partner.

7. The Honey Note

Write your partner's name on a piece of paper. Dab it with honey. Fold it toward you and tuck it into a small jar. This "seals" sweetness into your relationship.

- *Tip:* Renew by adding a fresh drop of honey every full moon.

8. Shared Tea Spell

Choose chamomile or rose tea. Brew one pot and share with your partner, holding hands around the cup before drinking. As the herbs steep, imagine peace and harmony infusing your relationship.

9. The Rose Quartz Stone

Place a rose quartz in the bedroom, or gift a small one to your partner. This stone, associated with Venus, radiates love and calm.

10. Knot of Patience

Tie a knot in a piece of string while thinking of patience and harmony. Place the string in a drawer. Whenever you feel irritation, hold the knot and remember: patience is tied into your relationship.

BINDING AND COMMITMENT RITUALS

11. Thread of Unity

Take two strings of different colors, one for each partner. Tie them together with three knots while saying: *"Bound by love, strengthened by trust."* Place in a safe box.

12. The Paper Heart Pocket

Cut a heart from paper. Write both names inside. Fold it and carry it in your pocket for seven days. At the end, burn it in a candle flame as a sealing act.

13. The Unity Candle

Light one candle together and both hold it while declaring your love. Allow it to burn completely, symbolizing unity and shared life force.

14. Shared Journal

Keep a journal where you and your partner write affirmations or dreams. The book itself becomes a sympathetic link holding your shared narrative.

15. Commitment Stones

Each partner chooses a stone and carries it for one lunar cycle. On the full moon, bury the stones side by side as a vow of continuity.

SELF-LOVE AND HEALING THE HEART

Love magic is not only outward-facing. One of the greatest acts of magical empowerment is learning to love oneself.

16. Mirror Affirmation Spell

Stand before a mirror daily. Say aloud three qualities you love about yourself. Touch the glass as though sealing those words into your reflection.

17. Rose Quartz Bath

Place rose quartz or pink stones in a bowl of water overnight. In the morning, pour the water into a bath. As you soak, imagine the water filling you with warmth and affection.

18. Chocolate Self-Offering

Eat a piece of chocolate slowly, dedicating it to yourself. Say: *"I am sweet, I am worthy, I am loved."*

19. Journal of Praise

Write daily notes praising yourself, as though you are your own beloved. These words become a living spell, reshaping your self-image.

20. Bouquet for the Self

Buy yourself flowers. Place them where you see them daily. Each bloom reminds you that you're worthy of beauty and care.

RELEASE AND LETTING GO

Love magic also helps us end relationships with grace.

21. Paper Burn Release

Write the name of the person you must release on paper. Burn it while saying: *"I release you, I release myself."*
Scatter the ashes.

22. Unknotting Ritual

Tie knots in a string while recalling moments of the relationship. Then slowly untie each one while speaking words of release.

23. Salt Water Wash

Add salt to a bowl of water. Wash your hands, saying: *"This connection is cleansed."*

24. Mirror Cut

Stand before a mirror holding scissors. Imagine the bond as a cord between you. Snip the air, symbolically cutting ties.

25. Farewell Planting

Write their name on paper, bury it under a new plant. The relationship is gone, but growth continues anew.

EVERYDAY LOVE PRACTICES

- Stir coffee clockwise in the morning while affirming: *"Love comes to me easily."*
- Place red or pink items in your wardrobe to signal openness to love.
- Dedicate a song as your "love charm" and play it often to raise your vibration.
- Use lipstick or chapstick with intention: each application is a ritual of attraction.
- Sleep with a lavender sachet to encourage peaceful love dreams.

REFLECTION

Love magic works best when it aligns with your real actions. Carrying a sugar packet under your pillow is powerful, but not if you close yourself off emotionally during the day. Sympathetic magic reminds us that small symbols shape the world, but we must live in harmony with the stories we are telling.

When we sweeten our relationships, we sweeten our speech. When we bind, we also commit to daily trust. When we practice self-love, we live in a way that attracts healthier bonds.

Love magic is not about bending others to your will—it is about harmonizing your world with the story of love you wish to live.

Chapter Five
Prosperity, Career, and Wealth

Prosperity is more than just money. It is the flow of resources, opportunities, and energy that sustains our lives. In sympathetic magic, wealth has always been represented by things that multiply—seeds, grains, coins, water—and by symbols of growth and flow. In a modern context, we can adapt those principles into objects we encounter daily: credit cards, pens, pay stubs, digital wallets, even apps on our phones.

This chapter provides a rich toolbox of charms and rituals for attracting prosperity, advancing careers, finding work, and maintaining long-term stability.

HOUSEHOLD CHARMS FOR ABUNDANCE

1. The Rice Jar of Plenty

Fill a clear jar with uncooked rice and keep it in the pantry or on the counter. Rice symbolizes countless grains, countless blessings. Each time you see it, say aloud: *"My resources multiply."*

- *Variation:* Add a few coins into the jar for financial blessings.

2. Coins in Shoes

Place a coin in each shoe before an interview or first day at work. Every step you take carries you toward wealth.

- *Variation:* Use pennies to "walk into opportunity," or silver coins for prestige.

3. Basil on the Windowsill

Plant a basil pot near your kitchen window. In folklore, basil ensures abundance. Water it regularly as an act of tending your prosperity.

4. Bread of Fortune

Bake bread and carve a symbol of abundance into the top before baking. Share the bread with family or friends to spread prosperity energy.

5. Green Button Talisman

Sew or carry a green button in your pocket. Its resemblance to coins makes it a quiet wealth magnet.

WORKPLACE AND CAREER MAGIC

6. The Dedicated Pen

Choose one pen only for signing contracts, writing applications, or jotting goals. Wrap it with green or gold thread when not in use.

7. Keyring of Opportunity

Add a new key to your keyring when beginning a job search. It symbolizes doors opening.

8. Sticky Note Sigils

Draw prosperity symbols on sticky notes and place them under your keyboard, chair, or monitor. These act as constant energetic reminders.

9. Business Card Blessing

If you have business cards, tap three times on the stack before handing them out, saying: *"Opportunity flows through these."*

- *Digital version:* Bless your LinkedIn profile picture by tracing a dollar sign on the screen.

10. The Coffee Charm

Before work, stir your coffee clockwise while focusing on productivity. Place three coffee beans in your wallet for drive and endurance.

FINDING WORK AND OPPORTUNITIES

11. Resume Candle

Place your printed resume under a green candle. Light the candle while visualizing your ideal job.

12. Doorway Invocation

Stand at your doorway, holding your resume or a note of intention. Step out with your right foot first, saying: *"I walk into opportunity."*

13. The Job Interview Coin

Carry a coin in your pocket during interviews. Rub it subtly when answering difficult questions to channel confidence.

14. Elevator Charm

If you work in a building with elevators, write "rise" on a small piece of paper and keep it in your pocket. Each ride up affirms your upward career journey.

15. The Prosperity Pen Holder

Keep pens upright in a cup on your desk. Pens symbolize writing your future—upright pens mean upward prospects.

Everyday Money Practices

16. Wallet Order

Keep cash bills in order, facing the same direction. A neat wallet signals to the universe that you respect money and can handle more.

17. Charging Credit Cards

Wave a green candle over your card and say: *"This brings wise spending and generous return."*

18. The Coin Blessing

Every time you receive change, bless it with gratitude before placing it in your wallet. Gratitude draws more.

19. The Daily Stir

When stirring soup, tea, or coffee, stir clockwise while stating: *"May my resources grow."*

20. The Purse Charm

Place a sprig of mint or a cinnamon stick in your wallet or purse to encourage constant inflow of money.

Long-Term Growth Rituals

21. The Goal Jar

Write financial or career goals on slips of paper. Place them in a jar with coins, rice, and basil leaves. Shake weekly to "activate" the goals.

22. Career Candle Monday

Burn a green or gold candle every Monday morning while setting weekly career intentions. Monday is ruled by the Moon, which governs growth and cycles.

23. The Prosperity Plant

Grow a hardy plant (like a pothos or jade). Each new leaf is a sign of your growing abundance. Tend it with care.

24. Coin in Honey

Drop a clean coin into a jar of honey. This symbolizes sweet, enduring prosperity. Place the jar near where you keep bills.

25. Calendar Charm

Mark the first day of each month with a prosperity symbol in your planner. Each month begins on a note of wealth.

PROTECTIVE PROSPERITY MAGIC

Not all money spells are about attraction. Some protect what you already have.

26. Salt Circle Wallet

Once a month, place your wallet inside a circle of salt overnight to clear negativity.

27. Protective Checkbook

Draw a protective sigil inside your checkbook or on your budgeting app background.

28. The Locked Box Ritual

Keep a small lockbox with a symbolic "seed" amount of cash. Never spend it. It becomes your financial anchor.

29. Garlic Threshold Charm

Place a garlic clove near your door. Garlic wards off loss and poverty.

30. Protective Coin Pair

Carry two coins bound together with thread. One represents wealth you spend, the other wealth you save.

DIGITAL PROSPERITY MAGIC

31. Phone Wallpaper Sigil

Design a prosperity symbol and set it as your phone's lock screen. Every unlock becomes a micro-spell.

32. Email Signature Affirmation

Add a small prosperity phrase to your signature: *"With growth and success."*

33. Playlist of Abundance

Create a playlist of songs that make you feel abundant, confident, and thriving. Listen before work or negotiations.

34. Banking App Blessing

Before opening your banking app, tap three times on the phone and say: *"Balance grows, flow increases."*

35. Charging with Screensavers

Use images of lush forests, overflowing bowls, or coins as screensavers to keep prosperity symbols constantly in your environment.

COMMUNITY PROSPERITY MAGIC

Prosperity expands when shared.

36. Coin in Fountain

When throwing a coin in a fountain, wish not just for yourself but for your whole community to prosper.

37. Shared Bread Ritual

Bake bread and give part to neighbors, saying: *"As I give, so abundance returns."*

38. Library Offering

Slip a dollar bill into a library book as a gift for the next reader. This keeps prosperity circulating.

39. Tip Generously Ritual

Whenever possible, tip slightly more than expected. Say silently: *"This generosity multiplies."*

40. Food Donation

Give food to a food bank with the intention that your household will never lack.

EVERYDAY PROSPERITY AFFIRMATIONS

- "Money flows to me with ease."
- "I respect money, and money respects me."
- "Each day brings new opportunities."
- "Abundance is natural, and I live in its stream."
- "I give and receive generously."

REFLECTION

Prosperity magic works by training your awareness. When you keep a rice jar, you see it daily and feel abundant. When you bless your wallet, you notice your spending habits. These charms are not mere superstition—they are symbolic practices that remind you to act in harmony with wealth.

Real prosperity comes when magic and action work together. Keep your wallet tidy, but also budget wisely. Stir your tea clockwise, but also apply for jobs. Grow basil, but also water your career with effort. Sympathetic magic amplifies your mindset, and mindset shapes how you move in the world.

Wealth is not just coins or bills. It is time, energy, opportunity, and connection. When you learn to live in prosperity consciousness, the symbols around you shift into allies, and the world opens doors.

Chapter Six
Protection, Cleansing, and Banishing

Where love and prosperity invite things in, protection and cleansing establish boundaries. Without protection, blessings leak away. Without cleansing, stagnant energies weigh us down. In sympathetic magic, protective charms often rely on objects with strong shapes (spikes, knots, mirrors), pungent smells (garlic, salt, herbs), or reflective qualities (shiny metals, glass). These qualities "stand in" for the invisible shield they create.

Banishing magic, meanwhile, is about release and repulsion. Where attraction magic pulls, banishing pushes. Old grimoires prescribed toads, black candles, or iron nails, but in the modern world, we can translate these principles into accessible equivalents: salt, vinegar, protective apps, kitchen spices, mirrors, even clothing choices.

This chapter explores dozens of methods for guarding yourself, your home, your finances, and your spirit in ways both traditional and contemporary.

EVERYDAY PERSONAL PROTECTION

1. **The Salt Pocket**

2. Place a pinch of salt in a small paper envelope or plastic bag and carry it in your pocket. Salt absorbs harmful energy.

- *Variation:* Use black salt (made with salt mixed with ashes or charcoal) for stronger repulsion.

2. Protective Keyring Charm

Attach a small charm shaped like a shield, lock, or key to your keyring. Keys naturally symbolize safety and guardianship.

3. The Red Thread Bracelet

Tie a red string around your wrist, knotting three times while saying: *"I am shielded."* The thread becomes a physical barrier to ill intent.

4. Pocket Mirror Deflector

Carry a small mirror. If someone directs negativity toward you, imagine it bouncing off the mirror and reflecting back to its source.

5. Sunglasses of Invisibility

Before entering a stressful environment, put on sunglasses and affirm: *"I am hidden from harm."* This modern charm uses concealment as a shield.

HOME AND HOUSEHOLD PROTECTION

6. The Threshold Sweep

Sweep the threshold of your door with a broom, always sweeping outward. This banishes negative energy from entering your space.

7. Protective Salt Line

Sprinkle salt along windowsills and doorways. This traditional charm creates an energetic "fence."

8. Garlic at the Door

Place garlic cloves in a small bowl near the entrance. Garlic's pungency is long associated with repelling danger.

- *Variation:* Replace cloves monthly so the energy stays strong.

9. Protective Plant Guardians

Grow protective plants like rosemary, basil, or cacti near entrances. They absorb and repel harmful energies.

10. Iron Nail Ward

Place an iron nail or small piece of iron (like an old key) above your doorframe. Iron has been used since ancient times to ward off harmful spirits.

DIGITAL AND MODERN PROTECTIONS

11. Password Sigils

Incorporate protective words or symbols into your passwords. Each login becomes an act of magical reinforcement.

12. Protective Wallpaper

Set your phone or computer background to a protective symbol—shields, circles, knots, or sigils.

13. Wi-Fi Blessing

Place a small bowl of salt near your router, asking that your digital connections be safe and clear.

14. Headphone Shield

Wear headphones (even without music) in public spaces if you need psychic protection. They act as a sympathetic signal of "do not disturb."

15. Protective Email Signature

Add a protective affirmation, such as "In safety and clarity," at the end of emails to subtly carry protective energy into communication.

Cleansing the Body and Spirit

16. The Salt Bath

Add a handful of salt to bathwater. As you soak, imagine negativity dissolving into the water.

17. Smoke Cleansing

Burn herbs like rosemary, sage, or bay leaves. Waft the smoke around your body, saying: *"I am cleansed, I am clear."*

- *Modern alternative:* Use essential oil diffusers if smoke isn't practical.

18. Shower Waterfall Ritual

Stand under the shower. Visualize the water washing away all negativity, carrying it down the drain.

19. Lemon Slice Cleansing

Rub a lemon slice on your hands. Lemon's acidity cuts through stagnant energy. Rinse with cool water afterward.

20. Clothing Shake

Before bringing clothes back into your room, shake them vigorously. Imagine dislodging clinging energies.

Cleansing the Home

21. Vinegar Wash

Wipe down surfaces with diluted vinegar. Vinegar's sharp scent drives away unwanted energy.

22. Floor Wash with Herbs

Boil rosemary and lemon peel in water, then use to mop the floor. This creates a refreshed, purified space.

23. Open Windows Ritual

Once a week, open all windows, clap your hands in each room, and invite fresh air to sweep the space.

24. Bell or Chime Cleansing

Walk through the house ringing a bell. The sound disperses stagnant or harmful energy.

25. Bowl of Salt Corners

Place small bowls of salt in room corners for 24 hours to absorb negativity. Dispose of outdoors after.

BANISHING NEGATIVITY AND ILL WILL

26. Freezer Spell

Write the name of a harmful influence on paper. Place it in a container of water and freeze it. The energy is symbolically "frozen out" of your life.

27. Vinegar Jar

Write the source of negativity on a slip of paper. Place it in vinegar with hot pepper flakes. Seal the jar and store far from daily life.

28. Lemon Cut Spell

Cut a lemon in half. Sprinkle with salt and leave on a plate to absorb negativity. Dispose of after a day.

29. Banishing Clap

Clap loudly three times while imagining harmful energy being broken apart and expelled.

30. The Shoe Stamp

Write a negative habit or influence on paper. Tape it to the bottom of your shoe and walk around all day, symbolically trampling it down.

PROTECTIVE CLOTHING AND ACCESSORIES

31. Black Clothing Shield

Wear black clothing when you need extra shielding. Black absorbs negativity and prevents it from clinging to you.

32. Hat of Concealment

Wear a hat to symbolically cover your crown (the seat of spiritual energy) in overwhelming places.

33. Protective Jewelry

Choose jewelry with circles, knots, or stones like obsidian or onyx. Each acts as a shield.

34. Sunglasses Against the Evil Eye

Wear sunglasses to deflect harmful glances—modern-day protection against the evil eye.

35. Protective Shoes

Dedicate one pair of shoes as your "armor." Whenever worn, they symbolize strength and protection.

PROTECTIVE FOOD MAGIC

36. Garlic Soup

Cooking and eating garlic soup strengthens inner defenses. Every spoonful becomes both nourishment and shield.

37. Cinnamon Tea

Cinnamon raises energy and dispels harm. Drink as a protective tonic before stressful days.

38. Salted Bread

Bake bread with extra salt sprinkled on top, serving as both sustenance and ward.

39. Protective Apple

Eat an apple while visualizing its skin as a shield around your own aura.

40. Hot Pepper Barrier

Keep dried chili peppers in the kitchen. Their fiery presence wards off malice.

NIGHTTIME PROTECTIONS

41. Protective Bedtime Prayer

Before sleep, say: *"Guard me as I dream, protect me as I rest."*

42. Under-the-Bed Salt

Place a small bowl of salt beneath your bed to absorb negativity while you sleep.

43. Dreamcatcher Modern Use

Hang a dreamcatcher or similar talisman near the bed to filter harmful energies in dreams.

44. Protective Pillow Sachet

Sew a small pillow sachet with lavender, rosemary, and bay leaves. Place under the pillow for restful, safe sleep.

45. Bedtime Stone

Hold a piece of obsidian or smoky quartz before bed, asking it to protect your dreams. Place it on the nightstand.

COMMUNITY AND SHARED PROTECTIONS

46. Protective Circle Gathering

When meeting with friends or family, sit in a circle and hold hands briefly, affirming collective safety.

47. Protective Meal

Cook a shared meal with garlic, rosemary, or onions—foods that protect all who eat them.

48. Neighborhood Salt Line

Sprinkle salt discreetly near your front step, with the intention of extending protection outward to the neighborhood.

49. Shared Chant

In a group, chant protective affirmations together. Shared voices amplify protective power.

50. Communal Candle

Light a candle in a safe space for collective protection, inviting blessings over the whole household.

REFLECTION

Protection and cleansing are not one-time acts. Just as you lock your doors daily, magical protection is most effective when practiced regularly. The beauty of sympathetic magic is its flexibility—you can sweep with a broom or swipe your phone screen with intention, and both can be acts of banishing.

Cleansing rebalances, protection maintains boundaries, and banishing removes what no longer serves. Together, they ensure that the love and prosperity you cultivate elsewhere in this book are safe and enduring.

Magic is not paranoia—it is self-care. It is the art of acknowledging that energies, like people, enter our lives constantly. Some are kind, some draining. With simple charms, rituals, and affirmations, you decide who gets to stay, and who is politely but firmly shown the door.

Chapter Seven
Health, Vitality, and Healing

Health magic has always been at the heart of sympathetic practices. In a world where access to medicine was once limited, people relied on symbolism, ritual, and natural objects to reinforce healing and resilience. Today we thankfully have modern healthcare—but sympathetic magic still offers support by strengthening our sense of agency, calming our minds, and aligning our lives toward vitality.

Healing magic does not replace medicine. It works alongside it, amplifying your will to recover, and reminding your body and spirit that you are resilient. Many traditional remedies used plants or animal parts unavailable today, but their symbols remain. A walnut resembled a brain, so it was used for mental clarity. A red thread looked like a vein, so it was tied to strengthen circulation. These associations can be reimagined with modern, accessible items.

Below are charms, rituals, and daily practices for physical health, emotional balance, recovery, and vitality.

GENERAL HEALTH AND VITALITY

1. The Apple a Day Charm

Eat an apple while affirming: *"Health is in me, health surrounds me."* Apples symbolize life force and daily renewal.

- *Variation:* Place apple peels in boiling water for a gentle "health tea."

2. The Walnut Brain Booster

Carry a walnut in your pocket when studying or needing mental clarity. Its resemblance to the human brain links it to cognitive strength.

3. The Lemon Water Cleanse

Drink warm lemon water in the morning. Imagine it washing toxins away and refreshing your body.

4. The Green Clothing Ritual

Wear green when you wish to focus on healing and vitality. Green is the color of growth and renewal.

5. The Health Jar

Fill a jar with whole grains, seeds, or beans. Keep it in your kitchen as a charm for strength and nourishment.

PROTECTION FROM ILLNESS

6. Garlic Talisman

Carry a clove of garlic wrapped in paper. Garlic has long symbolized resistance against sickness and decay.

7. Salt Water Wash

Rinse your hands with salt water when coming home, imagining all harmful energy being washed away.

8. Threshold Herbs

Hang rosemary or bay leaves near your door. These herbs act as guardians against illness entering your home.

9. Protective Soap Charm

Dedicate a bar of soap to health. Each time you wash with it, affirm: *"I cleanse away harm."*

10. The Umbrella Shield

Use your umbrella not only against rain but as a symbolic protective dome. When walking in crowded places, imagine it shielding your aura.

RECOVERY AND RENEWAL

11. Candle of Restoration

Light a white candle during recovery, saying: *"As this flame shines, so my strength returns."*

12. Healing Sleep Sachet

Place lavender, chamomile, and rose petals in a sachet under your pillow to encourage restorative sleep.

13. Spoon of Healing

Keep a wooden spoon in your kitchen only for stirring healing foods (soups, teas). The spoon becomes a sympathetic tool for nurturing.

14. The Warm Blanket Charm

Dedicate a favorite blanket to recovery. Each time you wrap yourself in it, imagine it sealing your body with healing warmth.

15. Healing Stones on the Nightstand

Place clear quartz or amethyst near your bed to radiate calming, restorative energy.

Mental and Emotional Health

16. The Walnut Writing Ritual

Write worries on paper. Crack a walnut and place the paper inside the shell. Bury it, symbolically "burying" the worry.

17. Tea of Peace

Drink chamomile or peppermint tea while journaling. The act becomes both physical and spiritual soothing.

18. Mirror Smile Ritual

Smile at yourself in a mirror daily, even if forced at first. This simple act shifts energy toward positivity.

19. The Music Charm

Dedicate a specific song as your "healing anthem." Play it whenever you feel low to re-anchor your energy.

20. Breath Counting Spell

Breathe deeply, counting seven in and seven out. Each exhale banishes anxiety; each inhale restores calm.

Boosting Energy and Vitality

21. The Citrus Carry

Carry an orange or lemon in your bag. Their bright colors and scents are life-affirming symbols of energy.

22. Jumping Ritual

Jump in place nine times while saying: *"I leap into vitality."* This quick burst reawakens sluggish energy.

23. The Red Sock Charm

Wear red socks when you need energy and drive. Red represents circulation, heat, and movement.

24. Sunlight Infusion

Leave a glass of water in sunlight for an hour. Drink it as a tonic, imagining you are ingesting light.

25. The Running Water Touch

Hold your hands under cold running water, saying: *"Energy flows into me."*

HOUSEHOLD HEALING PRACTICES

26. Healing Soup Ritual

When making soup, stir clockwise while saying: *"With each stir, health is restored."*

27. Candle in the Window

Place a candle in the window for an ill household member, symbolizing light guiding them back to health.

28. Fruit Bowl Charm

Keep a full bowl of fresh fruit on the table as a living charm for nourishment and vitality.

29. Salt in the Bath Corner

Place a bowl of salt in the bathroom corner to absorb sickness energy during showers or baths.

30. Health Calendar

Mark healing affirmations in your daily planner: *"Strength increases," "Energy flows," "I am restoring."*

Banishing Illness and Weakness

31. Onion Peel Charm

Peel an onion, place the skins in boiling water, then dispose outdoors. Symbolically discards illness energy.

32. Paper Body Outline

Draw a simple outline of your body on paper. Write illness or pain inside the shape. Burn the paper as a banishing act.

33. Candle Wax Drop

Drip wax into water while saying: *"As this melts, sickness melts away."*

34. The Feather Breath

Hold a feather. Blow across it, imagining illness leaving with each breath. Release the feather outdoors.

35. Freezer Banishing

Write the illness or symptom on paper. Place in the freezer to "freeze" its influence.

Self-Love and Preventive Health

36. Morning Gratitude Glass

Drink a glass of water upon waking. Say: *"I welcome vitality."* Gratitude begins the day in balance.

37. Daily Stretch Ritual

Stretch with intention, imagining your body lengthening like a tree reaching for light.

38. The Sun Spell

Stand in the sun. Feel its warmth on your skin. Say "as the sun shines, so do I."

39. Grounding Spell

Stand barefoot on the grass, imagining yourself rooted like a tree with roots going deep into the earth, attaining nourishment and goodness. Then see the tree flourishing, saying: *"And so I flourish."*

40. Rose Petals in the Bath

Put rose petals in the bath to affirm love and acceptance for your body. No bathtub? Scatter them on your bed.

GROUP HEALING & COMMUNITY RITUALS

41. Shared Healing Candle

Light one candle in a group, each person adding a spoken intention for healing.

42. Food Offering of Strength

Cook a meal for a sick friend, stirring health into every step.

43. Healing Circle

Sit in a circle holding hands, chanting words like *"strength"* or *"restore."*

44. Community Planting

Plant herbs together, dedicating growth to shared health.

45. Group Walking Ritual

Take a walk with others, affirming each step as a path toward wellness.

REFLECTION

Healing magic is not about controlling the body, but reminding it of its natural rhythm: to restore, to regenerate, to grow. Sympathetic charms—an apple for vitality, a walnut for clarity, salt for cleansing—act as physical reminders that the body is capable of balance.

Combined with medical care, rest, and nourishment, these practices empower us to engage in our own healing journey. They shift our mindset from passivity to participation. Each sip of lemon water, each red sock worn with intent, each smile in the mirror becomes a declaration: *I am alive, I am resilient, I am healing.*

Chapter Eight
Divination, Intuition, Connection

Divination is the art of perceiving patterns, signs, and symbols to understand what lies hidden—whether in the present moment, in unseen realms, or in the flow of the future. In sympathetic magic, divination is less about fortune-telling and more about *pattern recognition*. We use symbols that resemble, reflect, or echo the situations we face, and then interpret them as guides.

Where old folk practitioners might have cracked eggs into bowls of water or read wax drippings in oil, we can now adapt the same methods with tea bags, coffee rings, smartphone screens, or shuffled playlists. Intuition itself is the sympathetic bridge between outer signs and inner knowing. The objects don't speak—the *relationship* between the object and your mind does.

This chapter explores a wide array of practices, both traditional and modernized, to strengthen intuition, connect with spirit, and read the signs all around you.

STRENGTHENING INTUITION

1. **The Morning Card**

Pull one tarot card or oracle card each morning. Even if you don't fully understand it, note the image and see how the day echoes it.

- *Variation:* If you don't own a deck, pull a random image from your phone gallery. Interpret its message.

2. The Coin Toss Reflection

Flip a coin when making a decision. Notice not only the result but your *reaction*—did you feel relief or disappointment? That's your intuition speaking.

3. The Pen Pendulum

Tie a string to a pen or necklace. Hold it steady and ask yes/no questions. Movement becomes a channel for subconscious wisdom.

4. The Dream Notebook

Keep a notebook by your bed. Record dreams immediately upon waking. Over time, patterns emerge.

5. The First Thought Exercise

Upon waking, note your first thought or image. Treat it as a message from your inner self for the day.

SIMPLE FORMS OF DIVINATION

6. Candle Wax Reading

Drip candle wax into a bowl of water. Interpret shapes formed as symbols of what is emerging.

7. Coffee or Tea Grounds

Drink tea without a bag, or coffee without a filter. Swirl the last drops and read the patterns left behind.

8. Cloud Watching

Lie down outdoors and interpret the shapes of passing clouds. This ancient practice awakens imagination and intuitive vision.

9. The Playlist Oracle

Set your music player to shuffle. The first song is your answer. Pay attention to lyrics, mood, or title.

10. The Book Flip

Open a book randomly, let your eyes land on a sentence. Interpret it as a message.

Signs in Daily Life

11. The Feather Sign

Finding a feather on your path can symbolize spiritual support. Note the color: white for peace, black for protection, grey for balance.

12. Number Patterns

Repeated numbers (111, 333, 777) often appear as synchronicities. Treat them as affirmations that you are aligned.

13. Animal Encounters

Notice repeated animal appearances—ravens for mystery, cats for intuition, dogs for loyalty, butterflies for transformation.

14. Unexpected Words

When you overhear the same phrase multiple times in a day, treat it as guidance.

15. Traffic Light Oracle

Use stoplights when pondering a decision. Green = go ahead, yellow = wait, red = reconsider.

Spirit Connection Rituals

16. Candle Flame Focus

Sit quietly before a flame. Ask a question and observe the flame—steady flame for yes, flickering or struggling flame for uncertainty.

17. Ancestor Glass of Water

Place a glass of fresh water on your altar or shelf to invite ancestral guidance. Replace daily.

18. Incense Offering

Burn incense and say aloud: *"This smoke carries my message."* Observe how it drifts—rising straight for clarity, curling for complexity.

19. Journal Conversation

Write a question with your dominant hand. Switch to your non-dominant hand to "receive" an intuitive reply.

20. Digital Candle Ritual

Light a virtual candle on an app or website. Treat it with the same reverence as a real flame.

SYMPATHETIC INTUITION EXERCISES

21. Stone Selection

Place several stones in a bag. Without looking, pull one. Interpret its weight, texture, or shape as an answer.

22. Color of the Day

Close your eyes, pick a colored marker or crayon. Wear or carry that color—it reflects the energy you need.

23. Seed Toss Divination

Throw a handful of seeds onto the ground. Observe their scatter for patterns: clusters for abundance, distance for separation.

24. Phone Scroll Oracle

Scroll through your contact list. Stop randomly. The name you land on carries symbolic meaning for your current question.

25. Cup of Water Ripples

Tap the surface of a still cup of water after asking a question. Watch the ripples for symbolic answers.

PROTECTION BEFORE DIVINATION

Divination opens doors, so always establish protection first.

26. Circle of Salt

Place a small circle of salt around your candle or cards before reading.

27. Protective Stone

Hold obsidian, hematite, or black tourmaline while divining.

28. Affirmation Shield

Say: *"Only clarity and truth reach me."* before beginning.

29. White Clothing

Wear a white scarf or shirt during divination to symbolize purity and protection.

30. Knock and Begin

Tap three times on the table to "clear the space" before starting.

INTERPRETING SYMBOLS

31. Shapes

- Circle = unity, completion.
- Triangle = growth, conflict, or decisions.
- Spiral = cycles and progress.

32. Colors

- Red = passion, urgency.
- Green = healing, money.
- Blue = calm, communication.
- Black = endings, boundaries.

33. Numbers

- One = beginning.
- Two = partnership.
- Three = growth.
- Four = stability.

34. Elements

- Fire = passion, danger, transformation.
- Water = emotion, flow, intuition.
- Earth = stability, health, money.
- Air = thoughts, communication.

35. Directions

- North = grounding.
- East = beginnings.
- South = energy.
- West = endings, intuition.

DAILY PRACTICES TO SHARPEN INTUITION

- Journal three synchronicities you notice each evening.
- Meditate for five minutes daily focusing only on breath.

- Before eating, pause and ask your body if it truly wants the food.
- Carry a small notebook to capture passing impressions, dreams, or omens.
- End the day by asking: *"What lesson did today teach me?"*

REFLECTION

Divination is not about certainties—it is about *dialogue*. When you drop wax in water, shuffle cards, or open a random book, you are creating a mirror for your inner knowing. Sympathetic magic provides the stage; your intuition provides the performance.

The goal is not to see the future carved in stone, but to engage with symbols that spark insight, clarity, and new perspectives. Intuition grows with use. The more you notice signs, the more signs appear. The more you trust your inner guidance, the louder it speaks.

Divination is ultimately about relationship: between you and the world, you and your spirit, you and the hidden layers of reality. Every feather, every candle flame, every shuffled playlist becomes a message in the language of magic.

Chapter Nine
Everyday Sympathetic Magic for Modern Life

Magic does not belong only to altars, rituals, or special nights under the full moon. Sympathetic magic thrives in the *ordinary*. Every moment of modern life is filled with symbols and objects that can become tools for transformation—if you approach them with intention.

Think of it this way: when people centuries ago tied knots in string or whispered charms into bread dough, they were using what surrounded them every day. We can do the same with coffee mugs, smartphones, headphones, car keys, sticky notes, or even social media feeds. What matters is the *symbolic connection*.

This chapter shows how to live magically not just in ritual spaces but in workplaces, kitchens, buses, meetings, grocery aisles, and glowing screens. Here you'll find dozens of practical ways to anchor health, love, prosperity, protection, and creativity into the very fabric of your day.

Morning Routines

1. The Mirror Blessing

When brushing your teeth, smile into the mirror and affirm: *"I begin today with clarity and strength."*

2. Shower Cleansing

Imagine all negativity from yesterday washing off your body and going down the drain.

3. Breakfast Charm

Sprinkle cinnamon on your toast or cereal, affirming: *"Sweetness and prosperity flavor my day."*

4. Sock Ritual

Put on socks or shoes with awareness: right foot first for moving forward, left for grounding.

5. Coffee Stirring Spell

Stir clockwise to draw in energy, counter-clockwise to release stress. Whisper your intention into the steam.

COMMUTING AND TRAVEL

6. Car Key Sigil

Draw a protective symbol on your keychain with marker or nail polish. Every ignition repeats the spell.

7. The Red Light Pause

At stoplights, breathe deeply. Treat the pause as sacred stillness.

8. Protective Headphones

Wear headphones on crowded trains not only for sound but as symbolic shields against psychic overwhelm.

9. Travel Coin

Keep a small coin in your wallet specifically as a "safe travel charm."

10. Commuter's Knot

Tie a small knot in your bag strap before leaving home, saying: *"I return safe."* Undo it upon return.

Workplace Magic

11. Desk Crystal Grid

Arrange small crystals (quartz, citrine, obsidian) in a pattern on your desk. They quietly radiate productivity, abundance, and protection.

12. Sticky Note Spell

Write affirmations on sticky notes: *"Focus flows through me."* Hide them under your keyboard or in a drawer.

13. Water Bottle Charm

Draw a symbol of clarity or success on your water bottle. Each sip becomes a micro-ritual.

14. Protective Chair Charm

Tape a sigil or protective word under your chair to ground you during stressful meetings.

15. Prosperity Pen

Dedicate one pen for signing contracts, invoices, or work-related papers. Wrap it with a green thread when stored.

Technology and Digital Life

16. Phone Lock Screen Magic

Set your wallpaper to an image that reflects your current goal: abundance, health, protection, creativity.

17. Charging Ritual

Each time you plug your phone in, say: *"As this charges, so do I."*

18. Calendar Magic

Mark moon phases or affirmations in your digital calendar. Treat reminders as magical nudges.

19. Password Charms

Incorporate affirmations or protective symbols into passwords (e.g., Prosperity2025!).

20. Playlist Rituals

Curate playlists for focus, energy, or love. Use music as sympathetic magic to shift mood and reality.

Food and Eating

21. Salt Blessing

Sprinkle a pinch of salt over your meal before eating, silently blessing it for health and protection.

22. Cutting Fruit Intention

When slicing fruit, imagine each slice as dividing stress or obstacles into manageable parts.

23. Stirring Soup Spell

Stir clockwise to draw in nourishment, counter-clockwise to banish illness.

24. Bread Charm

When buttering bread, spread from center outward, symbolizing expansion of blessings.

25. Tea Bag Oracle

Ask a question while dipping a tea bag into hot water. Notice how quickly it sinks, rises, or floats for symbolic guidance.

Money and Errands

26. Grocery Abundance Ritual

Thank each item as you place it in your cart: *"I am nourished. I am abundant."*

27. Receipt Magic

Write "Paid and blessed" on receipts before discarding, sealing gratitude into the exchange.

28. ATM Blessing

Tap the ATM three times before use, saying: *"Wealth flows with wisdom."*

29. Coin Offering

Leave a coin discreetly in a public place with the thought: *"Abundance circulates."*

30. Wallet Order Ritual

Keep bills neat and facing the same direction to signal respect for money.

Social Interactions

31. Handshake Magic

Before a handshake, silently affirm: *"This exchange is fair and balanced."*

32. Compliment Spell

Offer genuine compliments as a form of sympathetic generosity: giving positivity ensures you attract it.

33. Protective Smile

Smile in tense interactions not just socially but as a shield of calm energy.

34. Text Message Charm

When sending texts, pause to infuse them with clarity or kindness.

35. Social Media Magic

Before posting, ask: *"Does this reflect the energy I want multiplied?"*

EVENING AND REST

36. Key Placement Ritual

Place keys in the same spot every night while saying: *"My path is clear tomorrow."*

37. Phone Cleansing

Swipe through notifications, deleting old ones as a banishing ritual.

38. Shower Reset

Evening showers can be symbolic "reset buttons," cleansing away the day's energy.

39. Gratitude Glass

Drink a glass of water before bed, naming three blessings aloud.

40. Pillow Affirmation

Whisper an intention into your pillow: *"Tonight I restore. Tomorrow I rise strong."*

MODERN MAGICAL SUBSTITUTES

Many old folk charms used objects that feel distant today—feathers, bones, live animals. Here are modern equivalents:

- Toad charms → frog keychains or plush toys.
- Animal bones → ethically sourced crystals or stones.
- Candles of beeswax → battery-powered candles

when fire is impractical.
- Knotted ropes → shoelaces, headphone cords, yarn bracelets.
- Herb bundles → essential oil rollers, scented candles, or even herbal teas.

The point is not the *material* but the *symbolic resonance*.

WEEKLY RHYTHMS OF EVERYDAY MAGIC

Monday (Moon):
focus on emotions, cleansing, self-care rituals.

Tuesday (Mars):
courage spells, workout charms, productivity boosters.

Wednesday (Mercury):
communication, learning, technology magic.

Thursday (Jupiter):
prosperity charms, gratitude rituals, expansion.

Friday (Venus):
love, beauty, friendship magic.

Saturday (Saturn):
protection, boundaries, banishing negativity.

Sunday (Sun):
vitality, creativity, clarity, solar blessings.

REFLECTION

Everyday sympathetic magic isn't about adding "extra tasks" to your day—it's about *infusing what you already do* with intention. You already stir coffee, scroll through your phone, commute, eat, shower, and sleep. With awareness, these become magical acts.

This is the heart of folk magic: turning the mundane into sacred. When you lace your shoes with intention, you are walking not just to work but toward destiny. When you delete emails as a banishing spell, you are practicing modern exorcism. When you sip water as a healing charm, you are in communion with life itself.

Magic is not rare. It is constant. And once you learn to live sympathetically, you will see every object, every action, every habit as a potential ally in shaping your reality.

Chapter Ten
Putting It All Together —
Crafting Your Personal Magical Practice

We have explored the principles of sympathetic magic, its ancient roots, and its modern applications. You've read about charms for health, love, prosperity, protection, luck, divination, and everyday life. Now, the final step is weaving these threads into a living, breathing practice that is uniquely yours.

No two magical lives look the same. Just as two cooks may use the same ingredients but create entirely different meals, so too will each practitioner of sympathetic magic shape their own craft. This chapter offers a framework for building your personal path—practical exercises, templates, and suggestions for integrating magic into your life in a way that is sustainable, joyful, and powerful.

Step One: Identify Your Magical Language

Sympathetic magic works through symbolism. To use it effectively, you must know what symbols speak most clearly to *you*.

Exercise:

- Write a list of five objects you encounter daily (e.g., keys, phone, coffee mug, shoes, notebook).
- For each, ask: what does this object symbolize to me?
- Decide whether that object could become a magical tool. For instance, your keys may represent opportunities, your mug nourishment, your shoes protection on your journey.

Over time, you will develop a personal lexicon of magical correspondences.

Step Two: Anchor Magic in Your Rhythms

The most effective spells are those you repeat naturally. Instead of designing elaborate rituals that disrupt your life, focus on *layering intention* into what you already do.

- Morning coffee = prosperity spell.
- Daily commute = protection charm.
- Bedtime routine = cleansing ritual.
- Weekly grocery run = abundance rite.

Exercise: Write down your daily schedule. Choose one magical act to weave into each major step of your routine.

Step Three: Choose Your Core Tools

You do not need hundreds of crystals, herbs, or books. Start with 3–5 items that hold deep resonance.

Examples of minimalist toolkits:

- A candle, a notebook, a stone, a spoon.
- A phone (digital spells), a key, a scarf.
- A deck of cards, a glass of water, a plant.

Your toolkit can be as simple as objects from your kitchen drawer. What matters is not extravagance, but *meaning*.

Step Four: Develop Signature Charms

Every folk magician had a "go-to" charm. These were not elaborate—they were the ones that worked, every time.

Exercise: Experiment with charms from this book. Notice which ones resonate. When you find one that feels potent, repeat it regularly. Over time, it becomes a "signature spell" in your repertoire.

Examples:

- A knot-tied bracelet for protection.
- Cinnamon in coffee for prosperity.
- Mirror affirmation for self-love.

Write your signature charms down in a dedicated notebook or digital file—your Book of Sympathetic Magic.

Step Five: Adapt, Don't Copy

Traditional folk magic used walnuts, toads, bones, and rare herbs because those were available. Today we adapt with what surrounds us.

Principle: The effectiveness of sympathetic magic lies in *symbolism*, not in historical accuracy.

- No mandrake root? Use a potato, carrot, or ginger—still human-shaped.
- No beeswax candle? Use an LED candle with intention.
- No sacred river water? Use tap water, blessed with your own words.

You are not "watering down" magic—you are keeping it alive.

Step Six: Record and Reflect

A magician is also a scientist: experiment, test, observe.
Keep a magic journal with these sections:

1. Charms Tried — describe what you did.
2. Outcome — what happened after.
3. Reflection — how it felt, what you'd change next time.

Over months, you will discover which charms consistently bring results.

Step Seven: Integrate Seasons and Cycles

Even in modern life, natural cycles influence us. Aligning with them strengthens your magic.

Moon Phases

- New Moon: beginnings, planting seeds.
- Full Moon: abundance, celebration.
- Waning Moon: release, banishment.
- Dark Moon: rest, inner work.

Seasons

- Spring: growth, love, health.
- Summer: prosperity, vitality.
- Autumn: protection, harvest.
- Winter: introspection, cleansing.

Personal Cycles

Pay attention to your energy. Track days you feel strong, tired, inspired. Work with your own rhythms.

Step Eight: Design Ritual Templates

Rather than memorizing dozens of spells, learn a *basic structure* you can adapt.

Template for a Sympathetic Charm:

1. Object: Choose something symbolically tied to your goal.
2. Action: Do something with it (tie, burn, bury, eat, write).
3. Words: Speak a phrase aloud, anchoring the intent.
4. Release: Place, wear, or dispose of the object as appropriate.

Example: For protection during travel:

- Object: shoelace.
- Action: tie three knots.
- Words: *"My steps are guarded, my path is safe."*
- Release: Wear the shoes until you return home.

This template can be used with any object, any goal.

Step Nine: Community and Sharing

Magic thrives in community. Folk practices spread through families, neighbors, and villages. In the modern world, communities exist online and in person.

- Share charms with friends—gift a knot, a crystal, or a blessing.
- Host a small seasonal dinner where each guest brings a symbolic offering.
- Join online groups, but remember: your intuition is the final authority.

Step Ten: Live as Magic

The ultimate goal is not performing spells occasionally but living sympathetically every day.

- When you see repeating numbers, smile—it's the universe winking.
- When you light a candle at dinner, pause for a moment of gratitude.
- When you delete an old email, imagine erasing clutter from your spirit.

The world itself becomes your altar. Life itself becomes your spell.

WORKBOOK SECTION:
Crafting Your Personal Practice

Use these prompts to build your system:

1. What three words describe what you most want from magic? (e.g., safety, love, abundance).
2. Which daily objects symbolize these things for you?
3. Which three charms from this book feel most powerful to you?
4. Write one simple ritual you could repeat weekly.
5. What cycle (moon, season, personal) do you feel most connected to?
6. How will you record your magical journey?

CLOSING REFLECTION

Sympathetic magic is not about imitating the past—it is about understanding the timeless human instinct to connect meaning with matter. A walnut once stood in for a wart; today a pimple patch does the same. A knotted cord once bound a prayer; today a shoelace holds our intention. A candle once flickered in a cottage; today a phone screen glows with the same focus of light.

You are part of a long lineage of humans who saw the sacred in the ordinary. With this book, you now carry that torch forward into the 21st century.

Remember:

- Magic is everywhere.
- Symbols are alive.
- You are the bridge between meaning and matter.

Live magically. Live sympathetically. And may every action in your daily life become a charm.

AFTERWORD

Magic, especially the kind that grows from the soil of everyday life, is not meant to be locked in dusty books or guarded in distant temples. It belongs in kitchens, in gardens, in pockets, and in the hands of those who live with intention.

Sympathetic magic is not about spectacle. It is about connection — seeing a walnut as a mirror of a wart, a candle as a spark of sunlight, a ribbon as a knot that holds a promise. The objects themselves are not "magical" in isolation; they are vessels. The power comes from the relationship you build with them, the symbolism you recognize, and the intention you pour into the act.

This book has given you hundreds of charms, rituals, and practices — some as simple as tying a thread, some as layered as full seasonal workings. They are not meant to overwhelm you but to show you how rich and abundant the language of magic is. Start small. Tie a knot. Drop a coin. Light a candle. Let these acts remind you that you are part of a world humming with symbolism, resonance, and pattern.

Whether you seek healing, love, prosperity, protection, or peace, remember this: the world has always spoken to us in signs and echoes. Sympathetic magic is simply the art of listening — and answering back with intention.

May the charms in these pages serve as stepping-stones. May you craft your own, adapting them as you grow. And may you never forget that the most powerful symbol you will ever carry is yourself: your will, your vision, your spirit.

APPENDIX A:
CHARMS FOR HEALING

Healing in sympathetic magic is about *restoring balance*. Folk healers didn't always aim to "cure" in a medical sense—they sought to draw out imbalance, strengthen vitality, and invite harmony between body, spirit, and environment. The same principles apply today. Whether you're dealing with stress, fatigue, illness, or heartache, these charms work by symbolically removing what harms and drawing in what heals.

Below are some healing charms, both traditional and modernized, ready to be practiced with readily available items.

CLEANSING & RELEASING CHARMS

- **Salt Bath Purification** - Dissolve a handful of salt in warm bath water. Imagine all illness or heaviness dissolving into the salt.
- **Shower Drain Charm** - As water runs down the drain, say: *"What does not serve me leaves me now."*
- **Candle Smoke Release** - Pass your hands through incense or sage smoke, pushing negativity away from your body.
- **Paper Burn Banishment** - Write the illness, stress, or pain on paper. Burn it in a safe container, releasing it as smoke.
- **Stone Carry & Release** - Carry a small stone throughout the day, imagining it absorbing discomfort. That night, place it outside on the earth to cleanse.
- **Apple Core Release** - Eat an apple slowly, imagining it filling you with health. Bury the core, symbolizing release of sickness into the ground.
- **Cold Water Splash** - Splash your face three times with cold water, saying: *"Vitality returns."*
- **Knotted Cord Release** - Tie knots in a cord, naming each worry or ailment. Bury the cord outside, letting the earth absorb it.
- **Mirror Exhalation** - Breathe heavily onto a mirror. Wipe away the condensation, symbolically clearing heaviness from the body.

- **Doorway Sweep** - Sweep the threshold of your room, saying: *"Illness out, health in."*

BODY & VITALITY CHARMS

- **Lemon Water Vitalizer** - Drink a glass of lemon water each morning to cleanse and refresh energy.
- **Cinnamon Tea** - A pinch of cinnamon in tea strengthens circulation and vitality.
- **Herbal Pillow Sachet** - Sew lavender, chamomile, and mint into a sachet. Place under pillow for restful healing sleep.
- **Warm Rice Compress** - Fill a cloth with warm rice. Press onto sore muscles to ease tension.
- **Healing Breath Count** - Inhale for four counts, hold for four, exhale for four. Repeat nine times.
- **Candle Flame Meditation** - Focus on a candle flame for five minutes to restore mental clarity.
- **Hand Over Heart** - Place your hand on your heart, saying: *"I mend. I heal. I strengthen."*
- **Honey Spoon Charm**
Eat a spoonful of honey, imagining it coating and soothing your body.
- **Healing Stretch** - Stand tall, reach upward, and imagine drawing energy from the sky into your body.
- **Ginger Footbath** - Soak feet in warm water with ginger slices for circulation and grounding.

HEALING THROUGH FOOD & DRINK

- **Soup Spell** - When cooking soup, stir clockwise saying: *"Health stirs into every drop."*
- **Garlic Amulet** - Carry a clove of garlic in your pocket to ward off sickness. Replace weekly.
- **Tea Blessing** - Hold your mug between both hands and whisper: *"Drink in healing."*
- **Fruit Offering** - Place fruit on your table as a symbol of vitality. Eat it mindfully, thanking the earth.

- **Milk & Honey Nightcap** - A warm glass of milk with honey invites peaceful, restorative sleep.
- **Mint Chew Charm** - Chew fresh mint leaves to refresh body and spirit.
- **Salt Circle on Plate** - Sprinkle salt in a circle around your meal for protection.
- **Healing Infusion** - Brew rosemary, thyme, and mint as tea to cleanse the lungs and uplift.
- **Orange Peel Pocket Charm** - Keep dried orange peel in a pouch for energy and vitality.
- **Bread Blessing** - Break bread at meals, saying: *"As this nourishes my body, so I am made whole."*

HEALING WITH NATURE

- **Tree Leaning** - Lean against a tree, imagining it drawing sickness from your body into the earth.
- **Flower Bath** - Add petals (rose, chamomile, calendula) to bathwater for soft healing energy.
- **Walking Spell** - Walk slowly outdoors, synchronizing breath with steps, whispering: *"Health in, illness out."*
- **Feather Healing** - Brush a feather gently along your arms and legs, imagining it sweeping away pain.
- **Sunlight Blessing** - Stand in sunlight for a few moments daily, affirming: *"Light fills me with life."*
- **Healing Rain** - If caught in rain, raise your palms, letting drops fall as a cleansing blessing.
- **Stone Circle** - Sit within a circle of stones for grounding and restoration.
- **Water Whispering** - Hold a glass of water outdoors. Whisper healing words into it, then drink.
- **Wind Exhale** - Face the wind and breathe out forcefully, imagining illness carried away.
- **Flower Vase Spell** - Keep fresh flowers on your table as a charm of renewal and growth.

HEALING THROUGH SYMBOLS

- **White Candle Healing** - Light a white candle for purity, placing it near the person in need.
- **Knot Untying Ritual** - Untie knots in a rope, saying: *"So too are blockages released."*
- **Circle Drawing** - Draw a circle on paper, place your name inside, and surround it with symbols of health (sun, leaves, water drops).
- **Mirror Affirmation** - Look into a mirror and say: *"I shine with wellness."*
- **Bell Ringing** - Ring a small bell to "shake out" stagnant energy from your space.
- **Ribbon Charm** - Tie a green ribbon around your wrist, charging it as a health amulet.
- **Healing Symbol Tattoo** - Draw a temporary healing symbol on your skin with marker or henna.
- **Circle of Hands** - Sit with friends or family in a circle, holding hands, chanting health affirmations.
- **Heart Drawing Ritual** - Draw a heart, color it green, and place it under your pillow.
- **Protective Word Stone** - Write the word "Heal" on a stone and carry it daily.

DREAM & SLEEP HEALING

- **Dream Sachet** - Fill a pouch with lavender, rose petals, and mugwort. Place under pillow.
- **Moonlight Bed Blessing** - Place bedding near a window to absorb moonlight overnight.
- **Glass of Water by Bed** - Place a glass of water near your bed to absorb sickness during the night. Discard in morning.
- **Sleep Affirmation** - Repeat: *"Each breath restores me"* until you drift into sleep.
- **Herbal Sleep Tea** - Drink chamomile or valerian root tea before bed.
- **Bed Corner Charm** - Place protective objects (stone, coin, herb sachet) at each corner of the bed.

- **Dream Journal Healing**
  Record dreams and look for guidance on what your body or spirit needs.
- **Soothing Sound Ritual** - Play calming music or nature sounds, imagining them weaving peace into your body.
- **Candle at Bedside** - Let a candle burn safely while you prepare for bed, symbolizing light guarding your sleep.
- **Under-Bed Charm** - Slide a piece of rosemary or sage under the bed as protection during healing sleep.

COMMUNITY HEALING PRACTICES

- **Shared Meal Spell** - Cook and share a meal, blessing it together with words of health.
- **Group Chant** - Chant a healing word in unison, letting vibration fill the space.
- **Healing Circle** - Sit in a circle, each person placing hands on the next person's shoulders, energy flowing around.
- **Candle Line Ritual** - Each participant lights a candle for the one in need.
- **Water Sharing Charm** - Pour water into a communal bowl, each adding blessings. Drink together.
- **Knitted Gift Spell** - Hand-knit a scarf, blanket, or item while focusing healing intent into each stitch.
- **Shared Writing Charm** - Each person writes a healing message, fold them together into a jar.
- **Singing Over Illness** - Sing softly over the person in need, letting music weave healing vibrations.
- **Community Prayer Beads** - Pass beads around a circle, each person adding blessings before returning them.
- **Gift of Flowers** - Give fresh flowers to someone unwell, affirming: *"As these bloom, so do you."*

PERSONAL HEALING RITUALS

- **Healing Bath with Crystals** - Place quartz or amethyst around a bathtub (not in water if porous).
- **Journal Release** - Write frustrations, then tear up the paper to release them.

- **Hand Washing Ritual** - Wash hands with intention: *"I cleanse my body, I renew my spirit."*
- **Body Oil Blessing** - Massage oil into skin with affirmation: *"Every cell strengthens."*
- **Pulse Point Anointing** - Apply essential oil to wrists, neck, temples while visualizing healing spreading.
- **Self-Hug** - Wrap arms around yourself, whispering kind words.
- **Laughter Healing** - Watch something funny deliberately, letting laughter be medicine.
- **Creative Healing** - Draw, paint, or write without judgment, as an outlet for pain.
- **Color Visualization** - Imagine green light filling your body, pushing out dull or grey shadows.
- **Healing Mantra** - Repeat daily: *"I am whole, I am strong, I am healing."*

Protective Healing Charms

- **Amulet Creation** - Wear a small pendant charged with the intent of health.
- **Green Thread Bracelet** - Tie a green thread around your wrist, knotting with affirmations.
- **Healing Stone Pocket** - Carry carnelian, aventurine, or jade. Touch when unwell.
- **Clothing Charm** - Wear green or blue clothing as a "health aura."
- **Protective Soap** - Carve a small sigil into a bar of soap. Use it for washing.
- **Salt Circle Around Bed** - Lightly sprinkle salt in a protective circle for recovery.
- **Shield Visualization** - Imagine a golden shield surrounding your body, repelling illness.
- **Handprint Charm** - Trace your hand on paper, draw protective symbols on each finger.
- **Healing Mask Ritual** - Before wearing a face mask (for illness prevention), bless it with intention.

- **Protective Scarf Charm** - Bless a scarf, saying: *"I am wrapped in healing warmth."*

Symbolic Healing Acts

- **New Clothes Ritual** - Wear fresh clothing to symbolize renewal.
- **Cutting Hair Charm** - Trim hair ends as a symbolic cutting away of illness.
- **Nail Clipping Release** - Dispose of nail clippings intentionally as shedding sickness.
- **Candle Wax Figure** - Melt candle wax into a small shape symbolizing your body, imagining it glowing with wellness.
- **Egg Absorption** - Rub an egg over your body to absorb illness. Dispose far from home.
- **Thread Burning** - Burn a thread to represent illness consumed by fire.
- **Sand Burial** - Write ailment in sand. Let waves wash it away.
- **Paper Boat Charm** - Write ailment on paper, fold into a boat, release into moving water.
- **Feather on Wind** - Release a feather, watching it carry illness away.
- **Smile Charm** - Smile deliberately, even when tired, as a signal of life returning.

APPENDIX B
CHARMS FOR LOVE & ATTRACTION

Love magic has always been one of the most popular forms of sympathetic practice. While medieval folk healers might have used hearts of doves or toad bones, in modern practice we look for symbolic equivalents that are ethical and accessible. The principles remain the same: like draws like, symbolism creates resonance, and intention shapes outcome. These charms are designed for romance, friendship, self-love, and strengthening bonds.

SELF-LOVE & CONFIDENCE CHARMS

- **Mirror Affirmation Charm** - Look into a mirror and say: *"I am worthy of love and I radiate it."*
- **Rose Petal Bath** - Scatter rose petals into a bath to bathe in self-adoration.
- **Strawberry Treat Ritual** - Eat strawberries, visualizing sweetness flowing into your heart.
- **Makeup Spell** - While applying makeup, whisper: *"I highlight my beauty, within and without."*
- **Clothing Color Charm** - Wear pink for affection, red for passion, or green for loyal love.
- **Candle of Self-Respect** - Light a pink candle, saying: *"I honor myself, so others may honor me."*
- **Perfume Enchantment** - Bless perfume with intent, spraying as though cloaking yourself in allure.
- **Jewelry Charging** - Wear jewelry blessed under moonlight as a charm of self-confidence.
- **Affection Tea** - Drink chamomile and honey tea to soften your self-criticism.
- **Smile Mirror Exercise** - Smile into a mirror daily to train yourself to radiate warmth.

ATTRACTING NEW LOVE

- **Rose Quartz Carry** - Keep rose quartz in your pocket to draw romantic opportunities.

- **Honey Jar** - Write your name and "loving partner" on paper, place in a jar with honey.
- **Apple Seed Charm** - Eat an apple, bury the seeds with intent: *"As this grows, so does love."*
- **Heart Drawing Ritual** - Draw two hearts interlocking, tuck it into your pillowcase.
- **Magnet Spell** - Carry a small magnet, imagining it pulling love toward you.
- **Sugar Sprinkle** - Sprinkle sugar in your shoes for "sweet steps" toward love.
- **Red Ribbon Knot** - Tie a red ribbon in a bow, visualizing romance tied into your life.
- **Love Letter to the Universe** - Write a letter describing your ideal partner. Seal it under a candle.
- **Moonlight Hair Charm** - Brush your hair under moonlight, saying: *"I glow with attraction."*
- **Scented Oil Pulse Points** - Anoint wrists with vanilla or rose oil before going out.

STRENGTHENING RELATIONSHIPS

- **Shared Candle Lighting** - Light a candle together, each saying a word of appreciation.
- **Handfasting Thread** - Tie a thread around both wrists briefly, symbolizing union.
- **Couple's Meal Blessing** - Cook together, stirring clockwise while naming blessings.
- **Rose Water Gift** - Spray rose water on shared pillows for harmony.
- **Joint Journal** - Keep a shared notebook where both write affirmations for the relationship.
- **Gift of Bread** - Bake bread for a loved one, symbolizing nourishment of bond.
- **Heart Stone Exchange** - Each partner gives the other a small stone, blessed as a token.
- **Photograph Blessing** - Place a photo of you together in sunlight to charge joy.

- **Ribbon Binding Charm** - Wrap two ribbons (red and white) together and knot them with intention.
- **Shared Bath Ritual** - Bath with rose petals and lavender, affirming unity.

REKINDLING LOVE

- **Candle Flame Divination** - Light two candles side by side; if flames lean toward one another, harmony grows.
- **Apple Halves** - Share an apple cut in half, symbolizing shared sweetness.
- **Music Charm** - Play your song together, dancing slowly to reignite affection.
- **Wine Toast Ritual** - Clink glasses, whispering: *"Our love deepens."*
- **Reweaving Ribbon** - Untie an old ribbon binding, retie it freshly to symbolize renewal.
- **Forgiveness Water** - Write resentments on paper, dissolve in water, pour away.
- **Joint Planting** - Plant a seed together, caring for it as your bond grows.
- **Shared Dream Sachet** - Sew herbs (jasmine, lavender) into a pouch, place under shared pillow.
- **Ring Recharging** - If wearing rings, cleanse in moonlight to refresh vows.
- **Hand-Holding Walk** - Walk together holding hands, chanting silently: *"We are strong."*

FRIENDSHIP & FAMILY LOVE

- **Yellow Candle Friendship Spell** - Light yellow candles when spending time with friends to invite joy.
- **Shared Meal Charm**
Bake cookies or bread for friends, infusing laughter.
- **Sunflower Gift** - Give a sunflower to symbolize loyalty and warmth.
- **Friendship Bracelet** - Tie colorful threads for each friend, each color representing blessings.

- **Circle Gathering** - Sit in a circle, each person naming one thing they value in another.
- **Shared Stone** - Pass a stone among friends, each blessing it, then keep it at gatherings.
- **Photo Frame Blessing** - Place group photos in a decorated frame, blessing it as a bond charm.
- **Family Meal Blessing** - Stand before eating, say in unison: *"We share love, we grow strong."*
- **Gift of Tea** - Give tea bags to friends, symbolizing comfort and togetherness.
- **Song Sharing** - Dedicate songs to one another, embedding love through music.

Love Divination Charms

- **Petal Counting** - Pluck petals saying: *"They love me, they love me not."*
- **Candle Wax Reading** - Pour melted wax into water, interpret shapes for love omens.
- **Dream Divination** - Place bay leaf under pillow, asking to dream of true love.
- **Key Under Pillow** - Sleep with a key under your pillow to unlock visions of love.
- **Pendulum Over Photo** - Hold pendulum above photo to ask questions of relationship.
- **Apple Peel Divination** - Peel apple in one strip, toss over shoulder; shape may form lover's initial.
- **Mirror Gazing** - Look into mirror by candlelight to glimpse future love.
- **Ring in Glass** - Drop ring into glass of water; bubbles or movements may indicate answers.
- **Flower Floating Divination** - Float two flowers in water —if they drift together, love prospers.
- **Star Gazing** - Ask stars to reveal guidance, count number of visible bright ones.

MODERN EVERYDAY LOVE CHARMS

- **Phone Case Enchantment** - Slip a rose petal or heart charm inside your phone case.
- **Digital Wallpaper Spell** - Set phone background to a symbol of love (rose, intertwined hearts).
- **Email Blessing** - Add a heart emoji intentionally when messaging loved ones.
- **Playlist Spell** - Create a playlist of love songs, charging it as an attraction magnet.
- **Lipstick Sigil** - Draw a sigil of attraction with lipstick on a mirror.
- **Social Media Charm** - Post a photo of yourself with roses or hearts to invite love energy.
- **Daily Jewelry Spell** - Bless earrings or necklace before wearing, affirming: *"I shine with love."*
- **Perfumed Bag**- Spray bag with rosewater to carry sweetness wherever you go.
- **Coffee Date Charm** - Stir sugar into coffee clockwise, visualizing sweetness between you and another.
- **Love Note in Wallet** - Keep a small folded paper with the word "Love" written on it.

STRONG ATTRACTION & PASSION CHARMS

- **Red Candle Passion Spell** - Light a red candle, focusing on desire.
- **Chili Pepper Charm** - Carry a dried chili to ignite passion.
- **Wine & Cinnamon Toast** - Toast with wine sprinkled with cinnamon for fiery romance.
- **Lingerie Blessing** - Bless lingerie by waving over incense before wearing.
- **Rose Oil Massage** - Massage with rose oil to heighten connection.
- **Kissing Spell** - Kiss under a doorway with mistletoe charm for heightened passion.
- **Strawberry Shared Dessert** - Feed one another strawberries as a symbol of indulgence.

- **Pomegranate Seeds** - Eat pomegranate seeds together to deepen intimacy.
- **Bed Linen Spell** - Sprinkle rose petals or lavender on sheets.
- **Candle Wax Hearts** - Drip candle wax in heart shapes, place under pillow.

BINDING & COMMITMENT CHARMS

- **Thread Binding** - Tie two threads together, naming the pair.
- **Knot in Ribbon** - Make knots symbolizing promises.
- **Vows in Candlelight** - Speak vows before a lit candle.
- **Joint Jewelry** - Wear matching rings or pendants as binding charms.
- **Handprint Ritual** - Trace both handprints on paper, overlay them, and keep safe.
- **Lock & Key Spell** - Gift a lock and key charm as commitment token.
- **Tree Carving** - Carve initials into tree with intent (ethically, without harming).
- **Shared Bracelet** - Each wear half of a matching bracelet set.
- **Photo Under Pillow** - Place partner's photo under pillow, binding dreams.
- **Promise Knot**- Knot thread while reciting vow.

HEALING HEART & RELEASING LOVE

Paper Heart Release - Cut paper hearts, write sorrows, burn safely.

Rose Petal Scatter - Scatter petals into moving water to release grief.

Forgiveness Candle - Light white candle, saying: *"I forgive, I free."*

Cutting Thread - Cut a cord to symbolize release of toxic bond.

Goodbye Letter - Write, then burn or bury.

Mirror Affirmation of Freedom - Say: *"I release the past and open to new love."*

Jasmine Bath - Soak in jasmine-scented water for healing heart.

Hair Cutting Charm - Trim hair ends to release old attachment.

Stone Throw - Throw stone into river, imagining burden carried away.

Self-Hug Ritual - Wrap arms around self, affirm: *"I love me most of all."*

APPENDIX C:
CHARMS FOR MONEY & PROSPERITY

Prosperity magic works on the principle of abundance attracting abundance. Like sympathetic healing and love charms, the goal is not just to "call cash" but to align yourself with the flow of opportunity, stability, and wise stewardship. In older traditions, charms might involve burying coins at crossroads or sacrificing animals. In a modern context, we replace these with ethical, symbolic acts using everyday objects that still hold the same resonance: coins, green herbs, flowing water, shiny objects, and growth symbols.

Below are prosperity charms to call wealth, luck in business, job security, and long-term stability.

MONEY DRAWING BASICS

- **Coin in Shoe** - Slip a coin into your shoe to "walk toward wealth."
- **Wallet Salt Charm** - Sprinkle a pinch of salt into your wallet to protect finances.
- **Green Candle Spell** - Light a green candle, saying: *"Money flows like flame."*
- **Rice Jar Abundance** - Keep a jar of rice in your pantry to symbolize never running out.
- **First Dollar Saved** - Frame your first dollar earned as a magnet for more.
- **Seven-Penny Charm** - Carry seven pennies tied in green cloth.
- **Sunlit Coin Charging** - Place coins in sunlight to charge with solar prosperity.
- **Basil Leaf Wallet Charm**
Slip dried basil leaf into your wallet for financial attraction.
- **Clove Prosperity Sachet** - Carry cloves in a pouch for luck.
- **Lucky Bill** - Keep a $2 bill or unusual coin as a permanent prosperity charm.

BUSINESS & CAREER SUCCESS

- **Desk Greenery** - Place a small plant on your desk to symbolize growth.
- **Business Card Blessing** - Sprinkle cinnamon lightly on business cards before handing them out.
- **Pen Charm** - Bless your work pen with intent: *"All I write leads to success."*
- **Resume Candle Ritual** - Place resume beneath green candle during job search.
- **Interview Coin** - Carry a shiny coin into interviews for confidence.
- **Calendar Blessing** - Mark calendar dates of meetings with a green circle.
- **Prosperity Coffee Stirring** - Stir morning coffee clockwise, affirming: *"Opportunities flow my way."*
- **Shoes Polishing Spell** - Shine shoes before important business, visualizing shining prospects.
- **Lucky Tie or Scarf** - Bless a piece of clothing as your "career charm."
- **Notebook Sigil** - Draw prosperity sigil on the inside cover of your work notebook.

HOME & HOUSEHOLD PROSPERITY

- **Coins in Jar at Doorway** - Place coins in a jar by the front door as a prosperity guardian.
- **Kitchen Cinnamon Stick** - Keep a cinnamon stick above the stove to attract abundance.
- **Bay Leaf on Window** - Place bay leaf on a windowsill for steady income.
- **Bowl of Oranges** - Display fresh oranges as symbols of gold and prosperity.
- **Prosperity Broom** - Sweep toward the center of the room to "sweep in" abundance.
- **Money Altar** - Arrange green cloth, coins, and a candle in one space for focus.

- **Jar of Lentils** - Keep lentils in a glass jar in the kitchen for ongoing food security.
- **Bread Baking Ritual** - Bake bread with intent: *"As this rises, so does my prosperity."*
- **Front Door Wash** - Wash doorway with salt water and cinnamon infusion to open way for money.
- **Shiny Object Display** - Place shiny coins or glass beads on shelves to "catch" wealth energy.

Candle & Fire Charms

- **Gold Candle Wealth Draw** - Burn gold-colored candles for abundance.
- **Double Flame Candle** - Light two green candles side by side, symbolizing money multiplying.
- **Coin Under Candle**
Place coin under candle holder during burning.
- **Bill Burning Spell**
Write "debt" on paper, burn it, releasing financial blockage.
- **Prosperity Incense**
Burn cinnamon or clove incense when focusing on finances.
- **Bonfire Offering** - Toss bay leaves with financial wishes into a fire.
- **Candle Wax Coins** - Drip candle wax into coin shapes, keep them in wallet.
- **Birthday Candle Wish** - On birthdays, always blow out candles with prosperity wish.
- **Flame Gazing** - Meditate on candle flame, visualizing yourself surrounded by abundance.
- **Lantern Light Charm** - Light lantern outdoors to "guide" money home.

Herbal & Food Prosperity Charms

- **Bay Leaf Wish** - Write wish on bay leaf, burn it.
- **Cinnamon Sprinkle** - Sprinkle cinnamon on morning toast.

- **Mint Infusion** - Drink mint tea for prosperity mindset.
- **Basil on Stove** - Keep potted basil near cooking area.
- **Nut Charm** - Carry hazelnuts for wealth attraction.
- **Bread & Salt Offering** - Offer bread and salt at table as abundance blessing.
- **Honey Jar for Finances** - Place coins in honey jar for "sweet money."
- **Almond Pocket Charm** - Carry almonds in pocket.
- **Sunflower Seeds Snack** - Eat sunflower seeds while visualizing money sprouting.
- **Coffee Bean Sachet** - Keep roasted coffee beans in pouch for luck.

PROSPERITY WITH WATER

- **Coin in Fountain** - Toss coin into fountain while wishing.
- **Running Tap Charm** - Hold coin under running water, saying: *"As water flows, so does wealth."*
- **Rain Collection Spell** - Collect rainwater, sprinkle around home for abundance.
- **Stream Offering** - Toss bread into stream as prosperity offering.
- **Bath with Mint Leaves** - Soak in mint bath for financial blessing.
- **Moon-Charged Water** - Charge water under full moon, drink to invite opportunities.
- **Water Glass Ritual** - Place glass of water with coin at bedside to "draw in wealth overnight."
- **Sea Salt Bowl** - Place bowl of salted water on altar to absorb poverty.
- **Lake Reflection Spell** - Look into lake, saying: *"Abundance reflects within me."*
- **Water Ripple Wish** - Toss pebble into water, make wish as ripples expand.

Everyday Prosperity Hacks

- **Credit Card Blessing** - Tap card three times before use, saying: *"Return threefold."*
- **Receipt Ritual** - Write "Paid in Full" on receipts.
- **Coin Jar Growth**
Start a coin jar with intent, never empty completely.
- **Morning Green Tea** - Drink green tea to align with prosperity.
- **Lucky Pen for Contracts** - Use same pen to sign contracts or checks.
- **Prosperity Shoes** - Clean shoes before job hunts or important meetings.
- **Digital Background** - Set phone wallpaper to abundance symbol (cornucopia, dollar sign).
- **Money Affirmation Alarm**
Set phone alarm label as: *"Wealth flows to me now."*
- **Jewelry Charm** - Wear gold or imitation gold jewelry as abundance magnet.
- **Citrus Wipe** - Wipe wallet with lemon peel for freshness and renewal.

Luck & Gambling Charms

- **Dice Carry** - Carry a pair of dice in pocket.
- **Lucky Number Note** - Keep paper with lucky numbers in wallet.
- **Four-Leaf Clover** - Press clover in book for gambling luck.
- **Rabbit Foot Substitute** - Use ethical charm (keychain, carved bone imitation) as luck talisman.
- **Casino Coin Charm** - Bless coin before gambling.
- **Left Shoe Coin** - Slip coin into left shoe for lucky ventures.
- **Game Card Blessing** - Bless deck of cards with prosperity oil.

- **Chili Pepper Charm** - Carry chili for fiery luck.
- **Singing Before Gambling** -mSing a money chant quietly before entering.
- **Slot Machine Knock** - Knock three times on machine before play.

Large Wealth & Long-Term Security

- **Tree Planting Prosperity** - Plant tree as a long-term investment charm.
- **Jar of Coins Buried** - Bury coin jar at edge of property.
- **Monthly Candle Ritual** - Burn green candle at start of each month.
- **Debt Knot Cutting** - Cut knotted string symbolizing debts.
- **Gold-Colored Bowl** - Keep gold-painted bowl on table.
- **Diamond Symbol Charm** - Draw diamond on paper, keep in wallet.
- **Savings Jar Sigil** - Draw sigil on jar where savings kept.
- **Bread Sharing** -Give bread to others to invite prosperity in return.
- **Plant Care Ritual** -Nurture plant daily, symbolizing wealth growing.
- **Lentil Soup for Stability** - Eat lentils at New Year for good fortune.

Symbolic Acts of Abundance

- **New Coin on New Moon** - Place coin on windowsill during new moon.
- **Gift of Coins** - Gift coins to children to circulate abundance.
- **Shiny Object Cleaning** - Polish shiny objects in home to "attract brightness."
- **Green Ribbon Wallet Charm** - Tie green ribbon around wallet.

- **Money Drawing Sigil** - Draw sigil on scrap of paper, keep in cash drawer.
- **Prosperity Stone** - Carry jade, citrine, or aventurine.
- **Feeding Birds** - Feed birds as offering, trusting abundance returns.
- **Cornucopia Symbol** - Place image or figurine of cornucopia on altar.
- **Gold Paper Charm** - Fold gold foil into shape (star, heart) and keep in wallet.
- **Smile at Money** - Whenever you receive money, smile to affirm welcome.

APPENDIX D:
CHARMS FOR PROTECTION

Protection magic is one of the oldest and most practical forms of sympathetic practice. Traditionally, people feared evil spirits, curses, and the "evil eye." Today, we face stress, toxic people, digital harassment, workplace hostility, and the invisible drain of modern living. Protection charms work by building boundaries, deflecting harm, and reinforcing personal strength.

Below are some modern protection charms, adapted from old folk practices and shaped for everyday use.

EVERYDAY CARRY CHARMS

- **Key Charm** - Carry an old key in your pocket to "lock out" harm.
- **Protective Coin** - Choose a coin minted in your birth year. Keep it as a shield.
- **Ribbon Bracelet** - Tie black or red ribbon around your wrist, knotting with protective intent.
- **Crystal Pocket Stone** - Carry obsidian, black tourmaline, or hematite.
- **Salt Pouch** - Keep a pinch of salt in small bag for warding.
- **Safety Pin Amulet** - Wear safety pin inside clothing to repel negativity.
- **Crossroads Dirt** - Collect dirt from crossroads in pouch. Carry for spiritual defense.
- **Iron Nail Charm** - Keep iron nail in bag or near bed (symbol of strength).
- **Herb Bundle** - Sew rosemary, sage, and bay into pouch.
- **Tiny Mirror Charm** - Carry mirror to reflect harm away.

HOME & HOUSEHOLD PROTECTION

- **Salt at Doorway** - Sprinkle line of salt across entry.
- **Broom by Door** - Keep broom bristles up behind front door.

- **Garlic Hanging o** Hang garlic cloves in kitchen.
- **Bay Leaf on Stove** - Place bay leaf near stove to protect home.
- **Red String Over Door** - Tie red string across top of doorway.
- **Protective Wreath** - Hang wreath with rosemary, pine, or protective herbs.
- **Bell at Window** - Hang small bell to ward spirits.
- **House Candle** - Burn candle in home weekly to maintain safe space.
- **Threshold Blessing** - Wash threshold with salt water and vinegar.
- **Protective Stone at Entry** - Place obsidian or onyx stone by front door.

CAR & TRAVEL SAFETY

- **Protective Keychain** - Add protective symbol (cross, hamsa, pentacle) to keychain.
- **Car Mirror Charm** - Hang small sachet of herbs from mirror.
- **Protective Sigil on Tires** - Draw sigil in chalk on car tires.
- **Coin Under Seat** - Place coin under driver's seat for safe journeys.
- **Road Dust Charm** - Sprinkle salt in car trunk for warding.
- **Travel Candle Blessing** - Before trips, light candle at home for safe return.
- **Bell in Car** - Hang bell to ring softly as protection.
- **Map Blessing** - Mark routes with symbol of protection.
- **Mirror Glance Ritual** - Glance in mirror before leaving home, affirming: *"I am safe."*
- **Water Bottle Protection** - Carry charged water bottle for vitality on road.

WORKPLACE & SOCIAL PROTECTION

- **Desk Salt Bowl** - Keep tiny salt bowl on desk.
- **Protective Pen** - Mark protective sigil inside notebook cover.
- **Coffee Cup Blessing** - Whisper into morning coffee: *"I am shielded today."*
- **Protective Headphones** - Bless headphones to block toxic words.
- **Keyboard Sigil** - Tape sigil under keyboard.
- **Paperclip Charm** - Bend paperclip into circle and keep in drawer.
- **Business Card Protection** - Sprinkle cinnamon on cards before sharing.
- **Protective Tie/Scarf** - Wear specific scarf as shield charm.
- **Mirror on Desk** - Place small mirror facing outward.
- **Protective Water Bottle Sigil** - Draw sigil on bottle with marker.

CANDLE & FIRE PROTECTION

- **Black Candle Shield** - Burn black candle to absorb negativity.
- **Circle of Tea Lights** - Surround yourself with circle of small lights.
- **Incense Smudging** - Burn sage, rosemary, or cedar.
- **Flame Visualization** - Imagine flame forming protective bubble.
- **Candle Wax Seal** - Seal charm bag with candle wax.
- **Lantern at Night** - Keep lantern lit as ward.
- **Red Candle for Strength** - Burn red candle on tough days.
- **Charcoal Bowl** - Burn charcoal as shield.
- **Candle Flame Crossing** - Pass hands through flame (safely at distance) to "cut off" bad energy.

- **Fireplace Blessing** - Throw herbs into fireplace for household protection.

PROTECTIVE FOOD & DRINK

- **Garlic Soup** - Eat garlic soup for warding from within.
- **Salt Water Sip** - Tiny sip of salted water for spiritual strength.
- **Cinnamon Tea** - Drink cinnamon tea for protective fire.
- **Bread Blessing** - Bless loaf of bread before baking: *"This nourishes and protects."*
- **Onion by Bed** - Cut onion placed by bed absorbs negativity.
- **Milk Blessing** - Drink milk with honey to coat self in sweetness and protection.
- **Apple Slice Charm** - Eat apple with affirmation: *"I am safe."*
- **Pepper Sachet** - Carry black peppercorns in pouch.
- **Lemon Water Cleanse** - Drink lemon water to cut negative ties.
- **Clove Chewing** - Chew clove for protective breath.

SYMBOLIC PROTECTION ACTS

- **Circle Drawing** - Draw circle around self on paper.
- **Mirror Facing Outward** - Hang mirror to reflect away harm.
- **Scissors Under Bed** - Place scissors under bed to cut nightmares.
- **Knife in Bread** - Stick knife upright in bread loaf to ward evil eye.
- **String Knot Spell** - Tie knots in string, saying each seals protection.
- **Egg Absorption** - Roll egg over body, dispose outside.
- **Shoes Crossed by Door** - Cross shoes by door to block entry.

- **Pin on Collar** - Wear pin to deflect curses.
- **Handprint Charm** - Draw own handprint, place on door.
- **Chalk Sigil on Wall** - Draw sigil in chalk above bed.

DREAM & SLEEP PROTECTION

- **Dream Catcher** - Hang dream catcher above bed.
- **Lavender Pillow Sachet** - Sew lavender sachet for restful ward.
- **Rosemary Under Pillow** - Slip rosemary sprig under pillow.
- **Salt at Bed Corners** -Place salt in small bowls at four corners of bed.
- **Protective Prayer Before Sleep** -Recite short protective prayer nightly.
- **Moonlit Bed** - Expose sheets to moonlight.
- **Water Glass Beside Bed** - Water absorbs negative dreams. Discard in morning.
- **Black Cloth Blanket** - Cover bed with dark cloth for protection.
- **Animal Totem Plush** - Bless plush toy as protective guardian.
- **Candle on Nightstand** - Light candle briefly before sleep.

DIGITAL & MODERN PROTECTION

- **Phone Case Charm** - Place small symbol under case.
- **Password Sigil** - Create password based on protective sigil.
- **Profile Picture Blessing** - Bless your online photo for shielding.
- **Inbox Salt Jar** - Keep salt jar near computer.
- **Headphone Protection** - Bless headphones as shield against gossip.
- **Charging Cord Blessing** - Wrap cord around crystal when charging phone.

- **Delete with Intention** - When deleting emails, affirm: *"This leaves my life."*
- **Protective Screen Background** - Set phone wallpaper to protective symbol.
- **Camera Eye Charm** - Place sticker over webcam with warding sigil.
- **Wi-Fi Blessing** - Name Wi-Fi network with protective phrase.

COMMUNITY & SHARED PROTECTION

- **Circle Chant** - Stand in circle, chant protective words.
- **Shared Meal Blessing** - Bless meal as shield for group.
- **Group Candle Ritual** - Each light candle, forming protective wall.
- **Stone Passing** - Pass stone hand-to-hand, charging it.
- **Shared Bracelet Ritual** - Each wear matching protective bracelet.
- **Singing Protection Song** - Sing together to raise protective energy.
- **Group Salt Circle** - Stand inside salt circle together.
- **Shared Water Bowl** - Bless water as group, sprinkle on each person.
- **Drumming Ward** - Beat drums to create shield of sound.
- **Shared Affirmation** - In unison: *"We are protected."*

APPENDIX E
CHARMS FOR LUCK & SUCCESS

Luck charms aren't about "random chance" so much as shaping probability in your favor. Sympathetic magic says: *like attracts like*. Carry a symbol of fortune, act out a ritual of increase, and you align yourself with favorable outcomes. In folk traditions, luck meant catching game, winning court cases, or surviving storms. Today, it can mean landing a new job, acing exams, winning competitions, or simply feeling that fortune smiles on you.

Below are some luck and success charms, each adapted for modern use.

PERSONAL LUCK CHARMS

- **Lucky Coin** - Carry a coin found on the ground heads-up.
- **Left Shoe Knot** - Tie knot in left shoe for good luck throughout day.
- **Morning Salt Rub** - Rub pinch of salt between palms to clear bad luck.
- **Lucky Jewelry** - Dedicate a ring, bracelet, or necklace as your fortune charm.
- **Three-Tap Ritual** - Tap doorway three times before leaving home.
- **Crossed Fingers** - Hold fingers crossed in pocket as portable luck charm.
- **Green Ribbon Charm** - Tie green ribbon around wrist for growth and luck.
- **Hair Talisman o** Braid own hair into thread, keep in pouch.
- **Stone in Pocket** - Choose smooth stone as luck anchor.
- **Hand Kiss Ritual** - Kiss palm before difficult task.
- **Gold Purse charm** - Have a gold color purse to set your intention to be wealthy.
- **Gold in Purse:** Put a small gold talisman in your purse or wallet to manifest 'gold' coming your way.

Luck in Love & Relationships

- **First Date Flower** - Carry tiny flower petal in pocket.
- **Handwritten Note Charm** - Write name of partner with heart, carry folded.
- **Rose Quartz Pocket Stone** - Carry rose quartz on romantic encounters.
- **Apple Slice Ritual** - Eat apple before meeting lover, visualizing sweetness.
- **Luck in Arguments** - Carry small clove of garlic in pocket to keep peace.
- **Hand Holding Knot** - Tie string around wrist before date, untie after.
- **Luck in Friendship** - Exchange small charm with friend.
- **Shared Meal Blessing** - Bless food for harmony and success in connection.
- **Photo Blessing** - Bless photo of partner with candle.
- **Shared Ribbon** - Both partners carry matching ribbon for mutual luck.

Luck in Study & Exams

- **Pen Blessing** - Bless pen before test, saying: *"All I write is correct."*
- **Notebook Sigil** - Draw sigil for success on cover.
- **Tea Study Ritual** - Drink peppermint tea while studying for clarity.
- **Desk Candle** - Burn candle during study to draw focus.
- **Sleep Stone** - Place amethyst under pillow night before exam.
- **Morning Affirmation** - Say aloud: *"Success is mine today."*
- **Lucky Socks** - Dedicate pair of socks for exams.
- **Bookmark Charm** - Bless bookmark used during study.
- **Fruit Ritual** - Eat orange before test to symbolize brightness.
- **Water Sip Charm** - Take sip of water before writing answers, affirm luck.

WORK & CAREER SUCCESS

- **Interview Coin** - Carry shiny coin to interviews.
- **Tie Blessing** - Bless tie or scarf with luck.
- **Desk Plant Charm** - Place plant on desk for growth.
- **Resume Candle Ritual** - Place resume under candle overnight.
- **Shoes Polishing Spell** - Shine shoes before important meetings.
- **Lucky Pen for Contracts** - Use same pen to sign contracts.
- **Desk Mirror** - Keep small mirror to reflect away negativity.
- **Sticky Note Sigil** - Draw sigil, stick under desk.
- **Daily Coffee Blessing** - Stir coffee clockwise with luck phrase.
- **Office Key Charm** - Bless office keys with protective luck.

MONEY LUCK

- **Rice Jar Charm** - Keep rice jar for abundance.
- **Cinnamon Wallet Blessing** - Rub cinnamon into wallet.
- **Coin Toss** - Toss coin in air, catch, wish for wealth.
- **Lucky Number Paper** - Carry paper with lucky number.
- **Bill Folding Ritual** - Fold money in triangle shape.
- **First Dollar Saved** - Keep first dollar of business.
- **Shoelace Coin Charm** - Tie coin into shoelace knot.
- **Money Jar Sigil** - Draw sigil on savings jar.
- **Sunlight Charging** - Leave wallet in sunlight.
- **Penny in Shoe** - Slip penny in shoe for walking toward wealth.

LUCK IN TRAVEL

- **Protective Keychain** - Add charm to travel bag.
- **Travel Candle Blessing** - Light candle before departure.

- **Coin Under Seat** - Keep coin under driver's seat.
- **Ribbon on Bag** - Tie ribbon on luggage for easy return.
- **Compass Sigil** - Draw compass symbol for guidance.
- **Travel Water Charm** - Carry small vial of water from home.
- **Bell in Car** - Hang small bell to ring during travel.
- **Footstep Luck**

Step first with right foot when leaving home.
- **Ticket Blessing** - Bless ticket or pass with intent.
- **Travel Snack Ritual** - Eat apple slice before trip for fortune.

GAMES & GAMBLING LUCK

- **Dice Carry** - Carry pair of dice in pocket.
- **Deck Blessing** - Bless deck of cards before play.
- **Lucky Number Chant** - Whisper lucky numbers before gambling.
- **Lucky Stone Knock** - Tap machine with stone before play.
- **Left Hand Coin** - Hold coin in left hand for luck.
- **Three Clap Ritual** - Clap hands three times before playing.
- **Green Shirt Charm** - Wear green for gambling luck.
- **Lucky Song** - Hum lucky song quietly before bet.
- **Four-Leaf Clover** - Carry clover in pocket.
- **Rabbit Charm (Ethical Substitute)** - Carry small carved charm instead of real foot.

SPORTS & COMPETITION

- **Shoe Knot Charm** - Tie shoelaces with lucky knot.
- **Sweatband Blessing** - Bless sweatband for performance.
- **Team Chant** - Create shared chant before game.
- **Water Sip Ritual** - Drink sip of water before playing.
- **Lucky Jersey** - Dedicate one jersey for luck.
- **Ball Blessing** - Bless game ball before play.

- **Wristband Sigil** - Draw sigil on wristband.
- **Hand Tap Ritual** - Tap ground three times before competition.
- **Sneaker Charm** - Slip herb sachet into sneaker.
- **Team Circle Spell** - Stand in circle, affirm success.

Luck for Creativity & Art

- **Brush Blessing** - Bless paintbrush or pen.
- **Notebook Candle Ritual** - Burn candle beside notebook.
- **Muse Invocation** - Whisper: *"Inspiration find me now."*
- **Colored Ribbon Charm** - Tie colored ribbon to instrument.
- **Tea with Cinnamon** - Drink tea before writing or painting.
- **Stone on Desk** - Keep quartz or citrine on desk.
- **Morning Sunlight Ritual** - Stand in sun, arms open, for inspiration.
- **Mirror Glance** - Look into mirror, affirm: *"I shine with talent."*
- **Paper Sigil** - Draw sigil, tape under sketchbook.
- **Lucky Socks for Stage** - Wear special socks during performance.

Daily Luck Rituals

- **Smile at Dawn** - Smile to rising sun.
- **Knock on Wood** - Knock three times to affirm luck.
- **Shoes Facing Outward** - Leave shoes pointing outward overnight for journeys ahead.
- **Morning Coin Toss** - Flip coin, catch, say: *"Luck is mine."*
- **Candle Flame Wish** - Blow out candle with wish.
- **Daily Salt Pinch** - Throw pinch of salt over shoulder.
- **Evening Gratitude Ritual** - List three lucky moments daily.

- **Hand Wash Spell** - Wash hands in cool water, affirm cleansing of misfortune.
- **Lucky Phrase** - Create personal phrase, repeat daily.
- **Pocket Stone Rub** - Rub lucky stone before leaving house.

Appendix F
Charms for Divination & Intuition

Divination is the art of peering beyond the ordinary and catching glimpses of the hidden. Sympathetic magic teaches that *like calls to like* — clear water reflects truth, shiny surfaces mirror hidden knowledge, and special tools sharpen the senses. In the past, witches might have used animal entrails, bones, or scarce herbs. Today, we can reach for everyday objects that hold the same symbolic weight.

Here are some charms and rituals to sharpen intuition, strengthen dreams, and bless divination practices.

TOOLS OF THE TRADE

- **Candle Flame Gazing** - Stare into a candle flame until images form.
- **Bowl of Water Scrying** - Fill dark bowl with water, gaze into reflection.
- **Mirror Charm** - Dedicate small mirror as "truth-seeing glass."
- **Crystal Charging** - Place quartz or amethyst on tarot deck overnight.
- **Divination Cloth** - Bless a cloth to spread under cards or runes.
- **Pendulum Thread** - Tie ring or pendant on thread; dedicate it as pendulum.
- **Ink Scrying** - Drop ink into water, interpret shapes.
- **Smoke Reading** - Burn incense, watch how smoke drifts.
- **Flame Twin Ritual** - Light two candles, see which burns faster for answers.
- **Salt Pattern Reading** - Sprinkle salt, read shapes left on surface.

DREAMS & NIGHT VISIONS

- **Mugwort Pillow Sachet** - Sew mugwort into sachet for dream clarity.

- **Lavender Tea Before Sleep** - Drink lavender tea to open dream visions.
- **Notebook by Bed** - Keep notebook to record dreams instantly.
- **Moonlight Pillow Blessing** - Expose pillow to moonlight before sleep.
- **Apple Seed Divination** - Eat apple before bed, ask for symbolic dreams.
- **Feather Charm** - Place feather under pillow for dream journeys.
- **Dream Water Glass** - Place glass of water by bed to "catch" dreams.
- **Night Candle** - Burn small candle before sleep, snuff it, then dream.
- **Mirror Under Pillow** - Slip small mirror under pillow for prophetic dreams.
- **Rose Petal Sachet** - Rose petals under pillow for love-related visions.

TAROT & CARD READING LUCK

- **Deck Smoke Bath** - Pass tarot cards through incense smoke.
- **Candle Over Deck** - Circle candle flame over deck for blessing.
- **First Card Blessing** - Before shuffle, draw one card, dedicate it to clarity.
- **Stone on Deck** - Keep quartz on deck when not in use.
- **Deck Storage Charm** - Wrap deck in silk or scarf.
- **Deck Knot Binding** - Tie ribbon around deck when resting.
- **Morning Card Ritual** - Pull one card daily for intuition training.
- **Tea Steam Blessing** - Hold deck over rising tea steam.
- **Card Edge Oil** - Lightly oil deck edges with rosemary or lavender.

- **Whisper to Deck** - Speak aloud: *"Guide me true."* before shuffle.

RUNES, STONES, & CASTING CHARMS

- **Rune Stone Charging** - Leave rune set in moonlight.
- **Casting Circle Ritual**

Draw circle before casting runes or bones.

- **Sand Reading** - Toss small objects on sand, read patterns.
- **Pebble Charm** - Mark pebbles with symbols for makeshift runes.
- **Clay Rune Making** - Carve runes into clay discs, fire or bake.
- **Coin Casting Divination** - Assign meanings to heads/tails or numbers.
- **Button Oracle** - Keep jar of old buttons, assign meanings, cast handful.
- **Shell Divination** - Use shells for yes/no answers.
- **Dice Oracle** - Roll dice, interpret numbers as messages.
- **Charm Bag Casting** - Fill bag with charms (keys, coins, beads), cast handful for reading.

EVERYDAY INTUITION BOOSTERS

- **Morning Water Ritual** - Drink glass of water slowly, listening for inner voice.
- **Breath Counting** - Count breaths until intuition arises.
- **Mirror Gaze** - Stare into own eyes in mirror for insight.
- **Walk in Silence** - Take walk without phone, listening for inner signs.
- **Feather Collection** - Pick up feathers, note meanings of colors.
- **Candle Drip Reading** - Drip wax into water, read shapes.
- **Kitchen Smoke Reading** - Watch steam rise from cooking pot.
- **Random Page Oracle** - Open book at random, interpret passage.

- **Music Shuffle Oracle** - Play music on shuffle, **interpret lyrics as answer.**
- **Phone Number Divination** - Notice repeating digits in daily life as signs.

Appendix G: Charms for Banishing & Cleansing

Banishing and cleansing rituals are the reset button of sympathetic magic. When the air feels heavy, when luck has soured, or when a space carries residue from past arguments, grief, or even illness, these practices cut away stagnant energy and restore clarity. In folk tradition, banishing often involved dramatic gestures — breaking pottery, throwing objects into rivers, or burning foul-smelling herbs. In modern practice, we translate the symbolism into safe, everyday actions that retain their potency.

Here are some charms and rituals for clearing away negativity, breaking ties, and freshening spiritual space.

SALT & WATER CLEANSINGS

- **Threshold Salt Line** - Pour line of salt across doorway to block unwanted energy.
- **Bowl of Salt Water** - Set bowl of salt water in room overnight; discard in morning.
- **Salt Water Hand Wash** - Wash hands in salt water after arguments.
- **Bath with Sea Salt** - Soak in salted bath to cleanse aura.
- **Sprinkled Corners** - Flick salted water into each corner of house.
- **Salt in Shoes** - Sprinkle salt inside shoes to shake off others' negativity.
- **Jar of Salt Under Bed** - Place jar beneath bed to absorb bad dreams.
- **Salt Circle Ritual** - Stand in salt circle, breathe deeply, visualize clearing.
- **Salt Pocket Charm** - Carry pinch of salt in pouch as personal purifier.
- **Sea Salt Candle Plate** - Place candle in dish filled with salt for combined fire-water cleansing.

Herbs & Smoke

- **Sage Smudge** - Burn sage to clear stagnant energy.
- **Rosemary Bundle** - Burn rosemary sprigs for protective clearing.
- **Cedar Smoke** - Waft cedar smoke in corners to drive out heaviness.
- **Incense Cone Banishing** - Burn cone of frankincense for sanctity.
- **Peppermint Smoke** - Burn peppermint for sharp cutting away.
- **Bay Leaf Banishing** - Write what you wish to remove on bay leaf, burn it.
- **Clove Smoke** - Burn cloves for protective clearing.
- **Juniper Wand** - Waft juniper smoke through rooms.
- **Paper Burn Ritual** - Write frustration on paper, burn, scatter ashes.
- **Candle Smoke Clearing** - Snuff candle and wave smoke around body.

Cleansing with Fire

- **Candle Flame Crossing** - Pass hands through flame (safely at distance) to burn away tension.
- **Bonfire Release** - Throw handful of dried herbs into bonfire, visualize release.
- **Matchstick Ritual** - Strike match, let it burn halfway, blow out, discard.
- **Ash Sweep** - Collect ash from fire, scatter outside to release energy.
- **Black Candle Absorption** - Burn black candle, let it soak up negativity.
- **Candle Drip Sealing** - Drip wax over paper naming what is banished.
- **Lantern Guiding** - Carry lantern through house at night to "chase out" shadows.

- **Candle Flame Scry-Banish** - Stare into flame, visualize what is leaving, then blow candle out sharply.
- **Charcoal Burn** - Burn self-lighting charcoal as symbolic purifier.
- **Candle Snuff Spell** - Snuff candle with spoken phrase: *"It is finished."*

WATER-BASED BANISHING

- **Running Tap Release** - Hold hands under tap, say: *"This flows away."*
- **Shower Visualization** - Imagine shower water washing off others' energy.
- **Rain Walk Ritual** - Stand briefly in rain to be cleansed.
- **River Stone Charm** - Throw stone into running stream to send away problem.
- **Ocean Offering**
Toss small bread piece into sea, release worry.
- **Water Glass Clearing** - Set glass of water on table during conflict, pour outside afterward.
- **Moon-Charged Water Wash** - Charge water under full moon, wash hands/face with it.
- **Bath with Lemon Slices** - Soak with lemon slices to cut ties.
- **Foot Wash** - Wash feet in water with rosemary.
- **Water Whisper** - Whisper frustration into bowl of water, flush down drain.

GESTURES & SYMBOLS

- **Clapping in Corners** - Clap hands loudly in corners to scatter stagnant energy.
- **Bell Ringing** - Ring bell to cut through heaviness.
- **Hand Waving** - Sweep arms outward from body to fling off bad vibes.
- **Floor Sweep Ritual** - Sweep house from back to front door, symbolically removing trouble.

- **Knocking Banishing** - Knock on wall or door three times, say: *"Leave me."*
- **Thread Cutting** - Tie knot in thread, cut it, releasing bonds.
- **Stone Toss** - Pick up stone, whisper problem, throw far away.
- **Window Opening** - Open all windows, invite fresh air.
- **Mirror Facing Outward** - Place mirror facing out to reflect negativity.
- **Foot Stamp** - Stamp foot, declare: *"Enough. Be gone."*

Appendix H
Charms for Friendship & Community

Human beings are social creatures; our bonds shape who we are. Sympathetic magic can nourish friendships, repair strained ties, and encourage new supportive connections. Folk traditions once relied on shared meals, knot charms, or exchanged tokens to bind allies together. In modern practice, we use simple gestures and symbolic items to represent unity, trust, and harmony.

Here are some charms for cultivating friendship, strengthening communities, and ensuring bonds remain warm and genuine.

CHARMS FOR ATTRACTING NEW FRIENDS

- **Sunflower Seed Carry** - Carry sunflower seed in pocket to attract cheerful company.
- **Cinnamon Tea Invitation** - Brew cinnamon tea when meeting new people; cinnamon draws warmth.
- **Orange Peel Pocket** - Carry dried orange peel to attract friendly encounters.
- **Smile Mirror Charm** - Smile into mirror before leaving home, "fix" it there.
- **Rose Quartz Pocket Stone** - Carry rose quartz to draw companions.
- **Apple Slice Sharing** - Offer apple slices to guests — symbol of friendship.
- **Handwritten Note Offering** - Write short kind note, slip into someone's day.
- **Keyring Token Gift** - Gift a small keyring as sign of opening doors between you.
- **Button Friendship Token** - Give a spare button to new friend; both keep one.
- **Sweet Treat Charm**
Offer candy or cookie in first meeting to sweeten bond.

Maintaining / Deepening Friendships

- **Friendship Candle Lighting** - Light candle weekly for friend, wish them well.
- **Shared Meal Blessing** - Say quiet blessing before meals with friends.
- **Rose Petal Jar** - Gift friend small jar of dried rose petals.
- **Knotted Thread Bracelet** - Braid thread bracelet together, each keep one.
- **Shared Playlist Ritual** - Exchange songs like charms, playlist as modern talisman.
- **Plant Gifting** - Give potted plant, both nurture it.
- **Shared Shells Charm** - Find two shells, keep one each.
- **Cup Exchange** - Gift mugs as bond tokens.
- **Friendship Pebbles** - Write initials on stones, swap.
- **Weekly Check-In Ritual** - Set recurring reminder to contact friend; ritual of continuity.

Healing Strained Ties

- **Lemon Water Wash** - Drink lemon water before reconciling conversation.
- **Apology Knot Untying** - Tie knot in string, untie it during apology.
- **Salt & Honey Charm** - Mix pinch of salt with honey, taste it: balance of bitter & sweet.
- **Shared Bread Ritual** - Break loaf of bread together after disagreement.
- **Forgiveness Candle** - Burn pink candle while thinking kindly of friend.
- **Mirror Empathy Exercise** - Look into mirror, imagine you are the friend.
- **Water Ripple Ritual** - Drop pebble into water, imagine ripples mending bond.
- **Olive Branch Offering** - Gift literal olive branch (or small leaf) as symbol of peace.

• **Rose Water Hand Wash** - Wash hands in rose water before reconciliation talk.
• **Joint Creation Charm** - Make something together (meal, craft) to rebuild connection.

CHARMS FOR COMMUNITY HARMONY

• **Circle of Candles** - Group gathers, each lights candle, circle forms bond.
• **Shared Potluck Blessing** - Everyone contributes dish = magical binding of community.
• **Ribbon Weaving Ritual** - Weave ribbons together as group, hang in shared space.
• **Stone Pile Offering** - Each add stone to pile = collective protection charm.
• **Community Bell Ringing** - Ring bell at gatherings to call harmony.
• **Joint Planting** - Plant tree or flower bed together as living bond.
• **Lantern Walk** - Each carries lantern in evening walk = shared light.
• **Song Circle Ritual** - Group sings refrain together, weaving voices.
• **Shared Water Pitcher** - Everyone drinks from same pitcher as unity ritual.
• **Story Exchange Night** - Each tells story — words as charms for connection.

TOKENS & GIFTS OF FRIENDSHIP

• **Friendship Coins** - Exchange coins; each keeps one.
• **Bookmark Exchange** - Gift bookmarks; bond in shared stories.
• **Charm Keychains** - Craft or buy identical charms, both carry.
• **Shared Candle Set** - Each takes one candle from a matching pair.

- **Notebook Exchange** - Swap notebooks filled with kind words.
- **Photo Stone Charm** - Glue small picture to stone, varnish it.
- **Twin Crystals** - Split pair of tumbled stones.
- **Message Jar Ritual** - Fill jar with notes of kindness, gift to friend.
- **Friendship Spoon** - Gift wooden spoon to symbolize shared meals.
- **Memory Token** - Pick up small object (leaf, ticket stub) during outing, both keep part.

Appendix I:
Charms for Confidence & Personal Power

Confidence is not arrogance; it is the inner flame that allows one to walk boldly, speak clearly, and pursue goals without shrinking from the world. Sympathetic magic uses bright, bold, fiery, and upright symbolsto strengthen self-assurance. Ancient folk might have used lions' teeth or warrior charms — today we rely on everyday substitutes that carry the same symbolic resonance.

Here are charms for courage, public speaking, overcoming fear, and radiating self-trust.

EVERYDAY BOOSTERS

- **Mirror Pep Charm** - Look into mirror, declare: *"I am ready."* three times.
- **Red Clothing Spell**
Wear red socks, scarf, or shirt to step into courage.
- **Lemon Slice Carry** - Carry lemon slice in bag for zest & freshness of spirit.
- **Straight Posture Ritual**
Stand tall, breathe deeply; body posture becomes spell.
- **Sunlight Walk** - Step outside, lift face to sun; soak in warmth = symbolic confidence.
- **Cinnamon Gum Charm** - Chew cinnamon gum before meeting; fire in mouth = fire in words.
- **Coffee Stirring Spell** - Stir coffee clockwise, say: *"Confidence grows with every sip."*
- **Peppermint Wash**
Wash hands in peppermint tea before job interview.
- **Button Charm** - Sew extra button into clothing as hidden reserve strength.
- **Coin in Pocket** - Carry shiny coin; shine it, imagine polishing your aura.

Public Speaking & Social Confidence

- **Apple Slice Ritual** - Eat crisp apple before speaking; crunch = clarity of voice.
- **Candlelight Rehearsal** - Practice speech in front of lit candle.
- **Throat Stone Charm** - Wear blue stone (sodalite, turquoise) at throat for clear voice.
- **Licorice Root Chew** - Chew small piece before speaking for strong voice.
- **Hand Symbol** - Draw small star on palm; press it before speaking for courage.
- **Knot Bracelet** - Tie knot in string bracelet; untie it after talk = tension released.
- **Clove Carry** - Carry clove bud in pocket; sharpness = clarity of thought.
- **Paper Sigil in Shoe** - Draw symbol of courage, place in shoe, stand upon it.
- **Rosemary Breath** - Breathe scent of rosemary sprig before entering room.
- **Sandalwood Oil Dab** - Dab sandalwood oil on throat for gravitas.

Charms for Overcoming Fear

- **Stone Toss Ritual** - Pick up pebble, whisper fear, throw it away.
- **Candle Fear-Burn** - Write fear on paper, burn in candle flame.
- **Salt Circle of Courage** - Stand in salt circle, declare fears leaving body.
- **Fear Knot Cutting** - Tie knot for each fear, cut string.
- **Fireplace Release**
Place written fears in fireplace, watch burn.
- **Shower Wash Away** - Whisper fears into water, let shower rinse them.

- **Mirror Affirmation** - Look in mirror, say: *"You are not small."*
- **Clay Break Charm** - Shape fear into clay lump, smash it.
- **Feather Blow** - Whisper fear into feather, release in wind.
- **Lantern Release** - Write fears, tie to paper lantern, release skyward.

Charms for Daily Courage

- **Morning Candle Ritual** - Light candle each morning, whisper: *"Today, I shine."*
- **Orange Slice Snack** - Eat orange for daily zest.
- **Shoelace Charm** - Tie shoelaces with intention: *"Each step is bold."*
- **Tea Steam Confidence**
Breathe steam rising, imagine inhaling courage.
- **Handwriting Spell** - Write name boldly on paper, underline three times.
- **Bold Color Pen** - Write notes in bright ink to remind of inner fire.
- **Clapping Ritual** - Clap hands three times before leaving house.
- **Candle Walk** - Walk holding candle in dark room; symbolic bravery.
- **Doorway Declaration** - Pause at door, say: *"I belong."*
- **Courage Coin Toss** - Flip coin, catch it, declare decision boldly.

Symbols of Strength

- **Lion Image Carry** - Carry lion picture, symbol of courage.
- **Dragon Drawing** - Draw dragon in notebook, reminder of fire inside.

- **Thunderbolt Symbol** - Wear jewelry with lightning motif.
- **Oak Leaf Charm** - Carry oak leaf = endurance.
- **Iron Nail Charm** - Carry iron nail = solid strength.
- **Phoenix Image** - Keep phoenix symbol near work desk.
- **Sword Symbol** - Small charm or even doodle of sword = decisiveness.
- **Crown Drawing** - Draw crown on paper, keep in wallet.
- **Mountain Stone** - Carry stone picked from high place.
- **Torch Symbol** - Sketch torch in journal; light of courage.

Appendix J: Charms for Peace & Sleep

Rest is the soil in which all other magic grows. Without peace of mind and restorative sleep, even the strongest charms falter. Folk healers once prescribed poppy seeds, dreamcatchers, and protective amulets; today, we adapt those traditions into gentle rituals and accessible symbols. These charms help calm nerves, ease tension, and invite restful dreams.

PEACEFUL HOME CHARMS

- **Chamomile Water Sprinkle**
Sprinkle chamomile tea in rooms to calm energy.
- **Rose Petal Bowl** - Keep bowl of dried rose petals on table for harmony.
- **Lavender Window Sachet** - Hang lavender sachet in window to invite peace.
- **Peace Candle** - Light white candle, say: *"This flame calms all who enter."*
- **Salt & Rice Bowl** - Set bowl of salt with rice to absorb quarrels.
- **Blue Ribbon Knot** - Tie blue ribbon to door handle for serenity.
- **Bell Charm** - Hang small bell on door; ringing clears tension.
- **Feather Vase** - Place feathers in vase to symbolize gentle air.
- **Wind Chimes** - Hang chimes; sound disperses disharmony.
- **Water Bowl Reflection** - Place water bowl in center of room to hold calmness.
- **Dove picture** - have a picture of a dove, a universal sign of peace.
- **Rainbow Fridge Magnet** - to bring hope.

CHARMS FOR INNER PEACE

- **Breath Counting Ritual** - Count nine breaths before stressful moment.
- **Pebble in Pocket** - Carry smooth pebble, rub when anxious.
- **Tea Stirring Charm** - Stir tea clockwise, whisper: *"Peace within me."*
- **Mirror Whisper** - Look into mirror, softly say: *"I am safe."*
- **Handwriting Flow** - Write worries on paper, tear and discard.
- **Peace Stone** - Carry blue stone (sodalite, lapis).
- **Rose Quartz Over Heart**
Hold rose quartz to chest while breathing deeply.
- **Candle Breath Ritual** - Blow candle out slowly, visualize exhaling stress.
- **Sunset Watch** - Watch sunset in silence; symbolic closing of day.
- **Hands in Warm Water** - Soak hands in warm water, releasing tension.

CHARMS FOR SLEEP PREPARATION

- **Lavender Pillow Sachet** - Tuck under pillow for restful dreams.
- **Chamomile Tea Ritual** - Drink chamomile tea before bed.
- **Moonlit Bed Sheets** - Expose bed sheets to moonlight before use.
- **Dream Journal at Hand** - Keep journal ready to receive dream messages.
- **Rose Water Face Wash** - Wash face in rose water before bed.
- **Feather Pillow Charm** - Place feather under pillow to counter light sleep.
- **Blue Candle Ritual** - Burn blue candle before bed, snuff when drowsy.

- **Counting Beads** - Hold string of beads, count to quiet thoughts.
- **Story Ritual** - Read aloud calming tale to self.
- **Mirror Covered** - Cover mirrors in bedroom for peaceful rest.

DREAM PROTECTION & SWEETENING

- **Dreamcatcher Charm** - Hang above bed to trap nightmares.
- **Salt Jar by Bed** - Keep small jar of salt near bed for warding.
- **Bay Leaf Under Pillow** - Slip bay leaf under pillow for prophetic dreams.
- **Apple Slice Snack** - Eat apple slice before bed for sweet dreams.
- **Honey Drop Ritual** - Taste honey before bed; honey attracts pleasant visions.
- **Protective Prayer** - Whisper: *"I am guarded through the night."*
- **Angel Figurine** - Keep figurine or image near bed.
- **Rose Quartz on Nightstand** - Promotes gentle dreams.
- **Candle Flame Meditation** - Stare at candle before bed, close eyes with image.
- **Cold Water Foot Bath** - Cool feet before sleep to relax body.

CALM AFTER CONFLICT

- **Shared Tea Ritual** - Drink tea with housemates after argument.
- **Peace Knot Ribbon** - Tie blue ribbon, hang visibly, declare quarrel ended.
- **Bread Sharing** - Break bread together, symbol of peace.
- **Joint Candle Lighting** - Both light same candle, sit in silence.

- **Circle of Chairs** - Arrange chairs in circle, sit and speak calmly.
- **Peace Water Spritz** - Spritz rose or lavender water around room.
- **Incense Offering** - Burn sandalwood after quarrel.
- **Window Opening Ritual** - Open all windows, invite fresh energy.
- **Shared Fruit Ritual** - Eat apple slices together to mend bonds.
- **Night Walk Together** - Walk under moon to cool emotions.

Appendix K: Charms for Warding Against the Evil Eye & Malice

The "evil eye" is one of humanity's oldest fears: the idea that envy or ill will can harm, whether intentionally or accidentally. From Mediterranean blue beads to Middle Eastern hamsa hands to Central European iron nails, every culture has devised charms to reflect, absorb, or deflect hostile attention. In sympathetic magic, we look for items that are watchful, reflective, or tough, capable of sending back or neutralizing malice.

Here are some powerful yet accessible charms to guard against envy, gossip, curses, and ill-meaning glances.

Reflective Charms

- **Mirror by Door** - Hang small mirror near entrance to reflect envy outward.
- **Pocket Mirror Carry** - Keep compact mirror in pocket to bounce energy back.
- **Shiny Coin Defense** - Carry polished coin to reflect ill will.
- **Mirror Fragment Charm** - Glue mirror shard to back of phone case as hidden shield.
- **Polished Spoon Token** - Keep small spoon in bag; polished metal as reflector.
- **Water Bowl at Window** - Bowl of water reflects negative gaze outward.
- **Silver Foil Packet** - Wrap small charm in foil, carry as mirror substitute.
- **Reflective Jewelry** - Wear jewelry with shiny surface — earrings, pendants, rings.
- **Crystal Sphere on Desk** - Place clear crystal ball to bounce away hostility.
- **Car Mirror Charm** - Hang small mirror in vehicle for road protection.

Absorptive Charms

- **Salt Bowl in House** - Keep bowl of salt to soak up malice.
- **Black Candle Burn** - Light black candle to absorb and neutralize envy.
- **Charcoal Piece Pocket** - Carry lump of charcoal; absorbs negativity.
- **Onion in Drawer** - Place onion in drawer to draw away gossip.
- **Egg Cleansing Ritual** - Roll egg over body, discard outside.
- **Clay Lump Absorber** - Hold clay lump, imagine it drawing malice, bury it.
- **Rice Bowl Offering** - Leave bowl of rice in kitchen overnight, discard daily.
- **Coal Box Ritual** - Keep small coal piece in box; replace monthly.
- **Soil Absorption** - Scatter earth on doorstep to ground envy.
- **Lemon Split Charm** - Cut lemon, sprinkle salt, leave near bed; discard later.

Protective Knots & Strings

- **Red Thread Bracelet** - Wear red string on wrist, traditional ward against eye.
- **Black Thread Ankle Charm** - Tie black string around ankle for stealth protection.
- **Knotting Ritual** - Tie nine knots in thread, carry with you.
- **Friendship Knot Exchange** - Tie knots in matching cords, exchange with ally.
- **Thread Across Doorframe** - Stretch thread across doorway as symbolic net.
- **Beaded Thread Charm** - Add bead to knotted string for layered defense.

- **Hair Knot Binding** - Tie own hair into knot, keep hidden in pouch.
- **Embroidery Protection Symbol** - Stitch protective pattern into clothing.
- **Shoe Lace Charm** - Tie extra knot in shoelaces for daily protection.
- **Woven Ribbon Shield** - Weave black and white ribbons together, hang nearby.

Eye Symbolism

- **Drawn Eye Charm** - Sketch eye on paper, keep in wallet.
- **Painted Eye on Stone** - Paint eye on pebble, carry in pocket.
- **Phone Wallpaper Eye** - Use digital eye image as protective sigil.
- **Blue Bead Eye Charm** - Wear traditional blue bead amulet.
- **Hamsa Hand Symbol** - Keep hand-with-eye drawing nearby.
- **Sunflower Eye** - Sunflower head resembles many eyes, keeps watch.
- **Clock Face Protection** - Place non-working clock facing doorway.
- **Eye Sticker on Bag** - Place cartoon eye sticker; playful, but symbolically potent.
- **Owl Image Charm** - Owl's eyes guard against hidden threats.
- **Peacock Feather Ward** - Feather's "eyes" stare back at malice.

Banishing Gossip & Malice

- **Chili Pepper Ward** - Hang dried chili peppers to burn away gossip.
- **Garlic String** - Hang garlic cloves in kitchen or near door.

- **Paper Tongue Ritual** - Draw a tongue on paper, cross it out, burn it.
- **Peppercorn Jar** - Fill jar with black pepper, keep near entry.
- **Shoes Crossed at Door** - Leave shoes crossed; symbolic blocking of envy.
- **Name-Freezing Charm** - Write gossip's name on paper, freeze it in water.
- **Vinegar Bottle Banish** - Fill jar with vinegar, drop in written slander, seal.
- **Silent Bell** - Keep bell tied so it cannot ring; binds harmful speech.
- **Clay Mouth Symbol** - Draw mouth on clay, smash it.
- **Whisper in Wind** - Whisper troubles into breeze, let wind scatter.

Appendix L:
Charms Against Spirits & Hauntings

Restless spirits, echoes of grief, or the residue of tragedy can cling to places and people. Folk tradition is full of remedies: iron nailed into thresholds, prayers spoken over water, the burning of foul herbs, or ringing of bells. The sympathetic principle is simple: loudness scatters, iron repels, light exposes, and sacred objects anchor. These charms give modern practitioners practical ways to secure their space.

Iron & Metal Charms

- **Iron Nail by Bed** - Place iron nail under mattress to anchor against spirits.
- **Key Under Pillow** - Iron key under pillow for safety in dreams.
- **Nail Cross** - Cross two nails, bind with thread, place at window.
- **Iron Horseshoe** - Hang over door, prongs upward, to repel spirits.
- **Scissors Open Under Bed** - Place scissors open under mattress; blades cut intrusions.
- **Keys at Door** - Hang bunch of keys by entrance to rattle spirits away.
- **Metal Spoon Charm** - Keep spoon on bedside table, reflective defense.
- **Iron Skillet Left Out**
  Leave iron pan visible overnight.
- **Nail Jar Ritual** - Fill jar with nails, shake when house feels heavy.
- **Pocket Key Charm** - Carry key in pocket when walking through haunted places.

Sound & Vibration

- **Bell Ringing** - Ring bell in each corner of room.

- **Clapping Ritual** - Clap loudly in darkened rooms to scatter shadows.
- **Drumming** - Beat simple rhythm on pot or table to break atmosphere.
- **Song Chant** - Sing repetitive chant to cleanse space.
- **Wind Chimes** - Hang at window, breezes carry protection.
- **Glass Tapping** - Tap glass with spoon, high tone drives spirits.
- **Door Knock Banishing** - Knock three times on inside of door, command "leave."
- **Hand Stomp** - Stamp foot, declare sovereignty of space.
- **Whistling** - Walk through house whistling bright tune.
- **Bowl Gong** - Strike metal bowl for resonance.

LIGHT-BASED CHARMS

- **Candle in Window** - Light candle, place in window as beacon of safety.
- **Lantern Walk**
 Walk through house with lantern to "chase" spirits.
- **Nightlight Protection** - Keep light on in hallway; symbolically denies darkness.
- **Candle Circle** - Circle of tealights around bed.
- **Flashlight Ritual** - Flash beam into corners, banish shadows.
- **Sunrise Exposure** - Open curtains at dawn to flood house.
- **Candle with Salt Ring** - Candle encircled with salt for pure light.
- **Fireplace Burning** - Burn logs overnight, fire protects.
- **Lamp with Blue Shade** - Blue light calms and drives away discord.
- **Mirror + Candle** - Candle before mirror doubles protective light.

HERBAL & HOUSEHOLD CHARMS

- **Garlic at Windowsill** - Place cloves on sill to ward intruders.
- **Rosemary Bundle Burned** - Waft smoke in rooms.
- **Mugwort Pillow Sachet** - Guards against night visitations.
- **Basil at Door** - Pot of basil near entry.
- **Bay Leaf Burning** - Burn bay leaves to banish.
- **Salt in Corners** - Sprinkle into each corner.
- **Onion Cut Ritual** - Halve onion, leave overnight, discard outside.
- **Vinegar Cup** - Cup of vinegar in room, sour scent clears space.
- **Peppercorn Scatter** - Scatter pepper where disturbances occur.
- **Juniper Smoke** - Burn juniper sprigs for old-style exorcism.

SYMBOLIC ACTS

- **Broom Sweep** - Sweep house outward, discard sweepings at crossroads.
- **Thread Net** - Hang knotted thread net by bed to catch intrusions.
- **Mirror Facing Door** - Mirror by door reflects spirits away.
- **Egg Rolling** - Roll egg over body, discard outside.
- **Paper Sigil on Door** - Draw symbol of banishment, tape to inside of door.
- **Crossed Sticks** - Place crossed sticks under bed.
- **Chalk Circle** - Draw circle on floor, sit within when anxious.
- **Bread Offering Outside** - Leave bread outdoors to appease restless dead.
- **Cold Water Splash** - Throw cold water at disturbance.
- **Commanding Words** - Speak aloud: *"You are not welcome here."*

Appendix M
Charms Against Bad Luck & Curses

Bad luck can cling like dust — sometimes from careless words, sometimes from curses, sometimes from simply feeling "jinxed." Traditional folk practice treats bad fortune as a weight that can be shaken off, washed away, burned up, or redirected. The principle is movement breaks stagnation, cleansing resets, and luck can be rebalanced by symbols of reversal or turning.

These charms help dissolve ill luck, whether it's from deliberate malice or from an accumulation of negativity.

Reversal Charms

- **Turn Your Clothes Inside Out** - Wear inside-out for a day to flip fortune.
- **Reverse Walking Ritual** - Take three backward steps, whisper: *"Luck turned."*
- **Upside-Down Broom** - Stand broom upside down to reverse misfortune.
- **Flip Coin Over Shoulder**
 Throw coin over left shoulder to dismiss curse.
- **Mirror Reversal** Hold mirror facing outward, command bad luck away.
- **Backward Knot** - Tie knot left-handed, untie to undo hex.
- **Wheel Symbol** - Draw circle with spokes, symbol of turning fortune.
- **Spinning Ritual** - Spin in place once to turn away ill fate.
- **Paper Arrow Charm** - Draw arrow backward on paper, carry it.
- **Turn Table Ritual** - Turn table or chair around, symbolically changing direction.

Cleansing & Washing

- **Salt Bath** - Soak in salted water to purify aura.
- **Rose Petal Bath** - Float petals in bath, wash away heaviness.
- **Egg Wash Ritual** - Rub egg over skin, discard far from home.
- **Running Water Release** - Stand by river, toss pebbles with worries.
- **Cold Shower Reset** - Quick cold shower, imagining luck clearing.
- **Soap Writing Ritual** - Write curse words on soap, wash until gone.
- **Rain Walk** - Walk briefly in rainfall to wash away misfortune.
- **Lemon Rinse** - Rinse hands in lemon water.
- **Milk & Honey Wash** - Wash face with mixture, sweetness restores fortune.
- **Smoke Bath** - Pass body through incense smoke.

Protective Carriers

- **Salt Packet in Pocket** - Carry pinch of salt in small cloth.
- **Garlic Clove Charm** - Clove in pocket repels curses.
- **Black Stone Amulet** - Carry obsidian, onyx, or any black stone.
- **Key on Chain** - Wear key as necklace, symbol of unlocking freedom.
- **Lucky Coin** - Keep coin found by chance as ongoing shield.
- **Four-Leaf Clover Substitute** - Carry paper clover if real one unavailable.
- **Knot in Cord** - Carry knotted thread to bind away bad luck.
- **Button Charm** - Sew extra button onto clothing for protection.

- **Seed Pod Token** - Carry seed pod; symbolizes renewal.
- **Rusty Nail in Pouch** - Iron breaks enchantments.

BANISHING RITUALS

- **Burning Paper Spell** - Write misfortune, burn paper in flame.
- **Bury Object** - Bury cursed item under tree.
- **Shoe Stomp** - Stomp shoes three times outdoors.
- **Whisper to Wind** - Whisper ill luck into breeze.
- **Candle Snuff** - Snuff black candle, ending cycle.
- **Garbage Toss** - Throw small object symbolizing curse in trash.
- **Hand Wash in Ashes** - Wash hands in ashes, then in clean water.
- **Spit Over Shoulder** - Ancient charm: spit three times.
- **Chalk Sigil at Door** - Draw protective sigil above doorframe.
- **Breaking Stick** - Snap twig, say: *"Curse is broken."*

RENEWAL & FORTUNE DRAWING

- **Wear New Clothing** - Symbolizes fresh beginning.
- **First Step Ritual** - Step with right foot when leaving house.
- **Bread Offering** - Offer bread outdoors, appeasing spirits.
- **Candle Blessing** - Light white candle, invite luck.
- **Lucky Meal** = Eat lentils, rice, or beans for prosperity shift.
- **Morning Sunrise Ritual** - Face east, breathe deeply three times.
- **Coin Gift** - Give coin away, generosity breaks misfortune.
- **Laugh Loudly**
Joy itself breaks bad luck's grip.
- **Wish Knot** - Tie wish into string, keep until luck changes.
- **Planting Ritual** - Plant seed, nurture it; symbolizes new cycle.

Appendix N: Charms for Creativity & Inspiration

Charms for Writers & Storytellers

- **Feather Pen Charm** – Write one word with feather before using regular pen.
- **Candle Muse Ritual** – Burn yellow candle, whisper: *"Bring me words."*
- **Notebook Under Pillow** – Sleep with blank notebook to catch dream images.
- **Walnut Inspiration** – Keep walnut on desk, symbol of hidden ideas.
- **Coin Toss Prompt** – Flip coin, let answer spark writing.
- **Paper Crumple Release** – Crumple paper of old draft, discard to clear mind.
- **Ink Dot Meditation** – Stare at dot of ink, imagine it expanding into story.
- **Book Under Chair Leg** – Sit balanced, grounding creative focus.
- **Alphabet Stone Toss** – Toss lettered stones for random prompt.
- **Ribbon Bookmark Spell** – Tie ribbon in notebook, charm for flow.

Charms for Artists & Makers

- **Brush Soak Ritual** – Soak brush in water overnight for fresh vision.
- **Color Candle** – Burn orange candle before painting.
- **Stone Palette** – Place pebble in paint water, stirring inspiration.
- **Random Color Charm** – Close eyes, pick random crayon; use it first.
- **Clay Ball Meditation** – Knead clay to shape new ideas.

- **Thread Knot Charm** – Tie knot in embroidery thread, start project.
- **Glass Jar Muse** – Keep jar of buttons, shells, or beads; shake for ideas.
- **Handprint Sigil** – Paint handprint on scrap paper, charm for originality.
- **Mirror Sketch** – Draw something while glancing at reflection.
- **Circle Doodle Ritual** – Draw circles until idea emerges.

CHARMS FOR MUSICIANS & PERFORMERS

- **Bell Ring Start** – Ring bell before practice to summon inspiration.
- **Coin in Pocket** – Carry coin, tap rhythm when stuck.
- **Whistle Charm** – Whistle new tune walking outdoors.
- **String Knot Ritual** – Knot guitar string offcut as talisman.
- **Songbird Feather** – Feather near instrument draws musical muse.
- **Mirror Practice Charm** – Play before mirror to reflect energy.
- **Water Glass Resonance** – Sing or hum into glass of water.
- **Drum Beat Offering** – Beat improvised rhythm to open flow.
- **Humming Walk** – Walk in circle while humming.
- **Candlelit Practice** – Practice by candlelight for altered mood.

CHARMS FOR GENERAL INSPIRATION

- **Stone Carry Charm** – Carry citrine or quartz for spark.
- **Morning Journal Ritual** – Write one word at sunrise.
- **Tea Leaf Reading** – Drink tea, interpret leaves for ideas.
- **Fruit Snack Ritual** – Bite apple before creating.

- **Hand Wash in Cold Water** – Refresh hands, reset energy.
- **Cloud Gazing** – Watch clouds for forms and metaphors.
- **Pebble Toss Game** – Toss stones, see where they land.
- **Mirror Word Spell** – Write word backwards in mirror.
- **Sunlight Walk** – Walk in morning light to stir thoughts.
- **Random Page Ritual** – Open book, use random sentence as spark.

BREAKING CREATIVE BLOCKS

- **Paper Rip Release** – Rip blank sheet dramatically.
- **Shout Ritual** – Shout outdoors, clearing block.
- **Cold Shower Reset** – Shock system into new ideas.
- **Silence Hour** – Sit without speaking, listen inward.
- **Odd Pairing Charm** – Place two unrelated objects together.
- **Number Roll Prompt** – Roll dice, let number guide theme.
- **Walking Backwards** – Stimulates fresh perspective.
- **Upside-Down Drawing** – Draw object upside down.
- **Nonsense Word Chant** – Invent word, repeat rhythmically.
- **Play with Shadows** – Shine light, trace shadow forms.

Appendix O
Charms for Fertility & Growth

CHARMS FOR PHYSICAL FERTILITY

- **Egg Under Pillow** – Symbol of life beneath rest.
- **Milk Bath Ritual** – Bathe in milk to invite nurturing energy.
- **Fruit Offering** – Eat pomegranate seeds as fertility symbol.
- **Seed Pouch Charm** – Carry small bag of seeds.
- **Carved Wooden Spoon** – Place spoon in kitchen as womb symbol.
- **Silver Ring Token** – Wear plain silver ring for moon fertility.
- **Moon Bathing** – Stand under full moon.
- **Honey Tasting** – Taste honey to sweeten conception.
- **Fertility Knot** – Tie cord with three knots, carry.
- **Flower Crown Ritual** – Wear crown of blossoms.

CHARMS FOR GARDEN FERTILITY

- **Bread Crumb Offering** – Scatter crumbs before planting.
- **Water Pouring Ritual** – Pour water in circle around seeds.
- **Sunrise Planting** – Plant seeds at sunrise.
- **Stone Marker Charm** – Place stone at garden's edge.
- **Ash Fertilizer Spell** – Mix ashes into soil.
- **Singing to Plants** – Chant while watering.
- **Eggshell Fertilizer** – Crushed eggshells for strength.
- **Coin in Soil** – Bury coin for prosperity.
- **Ribbon-Tied Stake** – Tie green ribbon to garden post.
- **Circle Walk Ritual** – Walk garden in circle, blessing.

Charms for Projects & Endeavors

- **Seed Jar on Desk** – Keep jar of seeds visible.
- **Notebook Egg Drawing** – Draw egg on first page of project notes.
- **Clay Ball Token** – Carry clay ball to symbolize shaping.
- **Wax Drop Ritual** – Drip wax on new work, sealing growth.
- **Ribbon Cutting Start** – Cut ribbon to begin project.
- **Sprouting Bean Jar** – Grow bean sprout visibly.
- **Circle of Pebbles** – Place around new idea notes.
- **Bread Slice Sharing** – Share bread before group endeavor.
- **Cup of Soil on Desk** – Soil cup draws growth energy.
- **Candle Lighting Ritual** – Light candle at project's start.

Charms for Relationship Growth

- **Shared Seed Planting** – Plant together.
- **Fruit Sharing** – Split apple or pear.
- **Thread Knot Ritual** – Tie cord together.
- **Watering Plant Jointly** – Care for one plant.
- **Gift of Greenery** – Give partner plant gift.
- **Mirror Dance** – Dance facing one another.
- **Bread Baking Together** – Symbol of shared fertility.
- **Double Candle Ritual** – Light two candles side by side.
- **Flower Exchange** – Swap blooms.
- **Paired Pebble Tokens** – Carry matching stones.

Charms for General Abundance

- **Corn Kernels in Bowl** – Symbol of harvest plenty.
- **Rice Scatter Ritual** – Toss rice outside door.
- **Milk Offering Outdoors** – Pour milk at base of tree.
- **Fruit Bowl Charm** – Keep bowl full of fruit.

- **Circle Dance** – Dance in circle to invite growth.
- **Honey Jar Ritual** – Keep honey jar visible in kitchen.
- **Bread Baking Offering** – Bake bread weekly.
- **Ribbon Around Vase** – Tie ribbon to vase of flowers.
- **Candle & Seed Ritual** – Place seed before lit candle.
- **Wish Whisper to Soil** – Whisper desire into soil before planting.

APPENDIX P
CHARMS FOR SAFE TRAVEL

CHARMS FOR JOURNEYS ON FOOT

- **Pebble in Shoe** – Carry smooth pebble for safe step.
- **Walking Stick Charm** – Carve mark on stick.
- **Thread Ankle Charm** – Tie cord on ankle.
- **Bread Crust Pocket** – Carry bread crust for safe path.
- **Whistle While Walking** – Keeps spirits at bay.
- **Sunrise Departure** – Begin journey at dawn.
- **Doorframe Touch** – Touch doorframe before leaving.
- **River Crossing Ritual** – Toss pebble into water.
- **Shadow Check** – Glance at shadow before departure.
- **Backwards Glance** – Look back once, then never again.

CHARMS FOR CAR TRAVEL

- **Iron Nail in Glovebox** – Wards misfortune.
- **Keychain Charm** – Add bead or feather.
- **Mirror Hang Symbol** – Hang protective item.
- **Salt Packet in Car** – Pinch of salt in dashboard.
- **Water Bottle Offering** – Keep bottle for spirits of road.
- **Horn Blessing** – Honk horn once before long drive.
- **Candle Bless Car** – Wave candle around car.
- **Ribbon on Antenna** – Tie colored ribbon.
- **Coin Under Mat** – Symbol of fortune under foot.
- **Bell in Car** – Small bell to jingle vibrations away.

CHARMS FOR SEA TRAVEL

- **Saltwater Bottle Charm** – Carry seawater in small vial.
- **Boat Knot Ritual** – Tie knot before departure.
- **Seashell Amulet** – Wear shell for protection.
- **Lantern Lighting** – Light lantern before boarding.

- **Fish Symbol Drawing** – Draw fish in pocket notebook.
- **Bread Toss Offering** – Throw bread to waves.
- **Anchor Symbol Charm** – Wear anchor design.
- **Coin Toss to Sea** – Toss coin for safe voyage.
- **Compass Carry** – Even if unused, symbol ensures direction.
- **Whistle Forbidden** – Avoid whistling on boats (old taboo).

CHARMS FOR AIR TRAVEL

- **Feather Token** – Carry bird feather.
- **Paper Airplane Ritual** – Fold, keep in bag.
- **Ribbon on Luggage** – Tied ribbon ensures safe arrival.
- **Cloud Drawing** – Draw cloud symbol on ticket.
- **Coin Toss Before Boarding** – Toss coin outdoors.
- **Water Bottle Under Seat** – Anchors flight.
- **Prayer on Takeoff** – Whisper protective words.
- **Window Touch** – Touch window frame.
- **Breath with Wings** – Inhale deeply, exhale as wings open.
- **Travel Pillow Blessing** – Sprinkle pillow with lavender.

CHARMS FOR RETURNING SAFELY

- **Stone from Home** – Carry stone from doorstep.
- **Ribbon Knot Untie** – Untie upon return.
- **Lamp Left On** – Leave light burning at home.
- **Key Carry Ritual** – Hold house key during journey.
- **Bread Loaf Waiting** – Leave loaf at home to "call back."
- **Salt at Threshold** – Sprinkle when departing.
- **Mirror Facing Inward** – Reflects traveler's image safely home.
- **Photo Carry** – Carry photo of home.
- **Thanksgiving Ritual** – Upon return, thank guides aloud.

APPENDIX Q:
CHARMS FOR SUCCESS & AMBITION

CHARMS FOR CAREER & PROMOTION

- **Pen in Pocket** – Carry pen to attract authority.
- **Desk Coin** – Place coin on work desk.
- **Ladder Symbol Charm** – Draw small ladder, tuck into planner.
- **Key Necklace** – Symbol of unlocking new roles.
- **Shiny Shoes Ritual** – Polish shoes before meetings.
- **Notebook Blessing** – Write goal three times in notebook.
- **Plant on Desk** – Growing plant symbolizes career growth.
- **Ribbon on Pen** – Tie red ribbon on pen for ambition.
- **Morning Mirror Affirmation** – Speak success aloud daily.
- **Bell Ring at Start of Work** – Signals productive energy.

CHARMS FOR EXAMS & LEARNING

- **Bay Leaf Under Pillow** – Aids memory.
- **Apple Slice Snack** – Boosts clarity.
- **Candlelight Study** – Briefly study by candle.
- **Knot Cord Study** – Knot cord while reviewing notes.
- **Peppermint Tea Ritual** – Clears mental fog.
- **Writing Sigil on Hand** – Write success symbol in pen.
- **Book Thread Bookmark** – Tie thread, bind knowledge.
- **Copper Coin Carry** – Copper sharpens intellect.
- **Salt in Pocket** – Keeps mind clear.
- **Study Walk Ritual** – Recite while walking.

Charms for Interviews & First Meetings

- **Lemon Water Wash** – Wash hands before leaving home.
- **Iron Key Pocket Charm** – Symbol of opportunity.
- **Button Polish Ritual** – Shine buttons or jewelry.
- **New Pen Ritual** – Carry unused pen for fresh start.
- **Candle Flame Gaze** – Focus on flame before leaving.
- **Ribbon Around Wrist** – Tie discreet ribbon for courage.
- **Hand Mirror Affirmation** – Speak confidence phrase.
- **Salt Sprinkle at Door** – Sprinkle behind as leaving.
- **Coin Flip Charm** – Toss coin to decide tie, shirt, etc.
- **Small Bell Token** – Carry bell to "announce presence."

Charms for Ambition & Drive

- **Red Thread Bracelet** – For energy.
- **Sunrise Walk Ritual** – Aligns with daily rising.
- **Candle Ladder Charm** – Burn three candles in row.
- **Peppercorn Pocket** – For fire and boldness.
- **Iron Nail on Desk** – Symbol of strength.
- **Mirror Glance Ritual** – Glance before action.
- **Stomp Foot Before Task** – Physical grounding.
- **Garlic in Drawer** – Keeps away office envy.
- **Circle Drawing Ritual** – Focuses intention.
- **Bread Bite Offering** – Bite bread before big task.

Charms for Ongoing Prosperity

- **Candle with Coin Base** – Burn candle on coin.
- **Weekly Plant Watering Ritual** – Aligns career with steady growth.
- **Ribbon-Wrapped Notebook** – Tied goals.
- **Peppermint Chewing Charm** – Chew mint before projects.
- **Iron Spoon in Kitchen** – Strengthens household ambition.

- **Quartz Stone in Pocket** – Clarity of purpose.
- **New Shoes Ritual** – First step in fresh shoes = progress.
- **Daily Bell Ring** – Morning signal of success.
- **Shared Bread Ritual** – Share food with coworkers.
- **Thanksgiving Offering** – Thank tools after each success.

APPENDIX R
CHARMS FOR COMMUNITY

CHARMS FOR BUILDING NEW FRIENDSHIPS

- **Shared Bread Ritual** – Break bread with new acquaintance.
- **Coin Exchange Charm** – Swap coins, bind connection.
- **Ribbon Tie Ceremony** – Tie cords together, exchange.
- **Flower Gift** – Offer bloom with intention.
- **Stone Swap** – Trade pebbles to carry each other's goodwill.
- **Handshake Affirmation** – Secret word whispered at handshake.
- **Fruit Sharing Ritual** – Split apple, pear, or orange.
- **Mirror Compliment** – Offer compliment as charm of recognition.
- **Candle Lighting Together** – Light single flame from two candles.
- **Circle Walk Ritual** – Walk in circle, symbol of unity.

CHARMS FOR MAINTAINING BONDS

- **Friendship Knot Bracelet** – Tie knot cord bracelets.
- **Monthly Meal Tradition** – Share meal on same day monthly.
- **Stone Jar Ritual** – Place pebble in jar each time you meet.
- **Thread Weaving Charm** – Weave threads into joint cloth.
- **Plant Exchange** – Gift living plant.
- **Photo Token Exchange** – Swap small photos.
- **Candle Pair Ritual** – Burn two candles side by side.
- **Story Exchange** – Each tells one memory to strengthen link.

- **Written Word Charm** – Write single word each, swap papers.
- **Joint Bread Baking** – Symbol of sustaining connection.

Charms for Group Harmony

- **Circle of Chairs** – Arrange chairs in circle for meetings.
- **Shared Drink Ritual** – Pour from same jug.
- **Group Candle Spiral** – Candles arranged in spiral, lit together.
- **Song Singing** – Shared song builds unity.
- **Clapping Rhythm** – Hands clapping together harmonizes.
- **Joint Bell Ring** – Everyone rings bell once.
- **Salt Bowl in Center** – Salt purifies group.
- **Bread Plate Passing** – Pass bread around, each takes piece.
- **Stone Circle Walk** – Place stones in circle outdoors, walk around.
- **Thread Web Ritual** – Pass ball of yarn, weave web between people.

Charms for Healing Broken Bonds

- **Ribbon Cutting Ritual** – Cut knotted ribbon to sever quarrel.
- **Shared Meal of Sweet Foods** – Eat honey, fruit together.
- **Apology Written Charm** – Write apology, burn paper.
- **Stone Toss in River** – Throw stone to release anger.
- **Salt Circle Conversation** – Sit within salt circle to speak.
- **Two Candles Rejoining** – Move two candles together.
- **Water Pouring Ritual** – Pour from one cup to another.
- **Gift of Bread** – Give bread to mend friendship.
- **Joint Planting** – Plant flower together.
- **Mirror Exchange** – Look into mirror together, forgive.

CHARMS FOR COMMUNITY STRENGTH

- **Lantern Walk** – Community walk with lanterns.
- **Bonfire Ritual** – Gather around fire, share wishes.
- **Circle Dance** – Traditional bonding.
- **Bell Ringing in Town** – Bells unite people.
- **Shared Feast** – Potluck as magical act.
- **Banner Weaving** – Each contributes to cloth banner.
- **Stone Cairn Building** – Group stacks stones.
- **Saltwater Sprinkling** – Sprinkle saltwater on community grounds.
- **Joint Bread Offering Outdoors** – Leave loaf for spirits of land.
- **Thanksgiving Chant** – Group chant of gratitude.

APPENDIX S
CHARMS FOR CONFIDENCE & PERSONAL POWER

CHARMS FOR DAILY CONFIDENCE

- **Mirror Smile Ritual** – Smile at self each morning.
- **Red Clothing Charm** – Wear red item.
- **Coin in Shoe** – Grounded power.
- **Stomp Ritual** – Stomp foot three times before leaving home.
- **Peppermint Chew** – Freshens words.
- **Salt Hand Rub** – Rub salt, wash off, leave doubt behind.
- **Small Stone Token** – Grip stone when nervous.
- **Hair Comb Charm** – Comb hair deliberately, charm of readiness.
- **Button Polish** – Shine buttons before event.
- **Shout Outdoors** – Release fear by loud sound.

CHARMS FOR SPEAKING & PERFORMING

- **Lemon Slice Lick** – Clears throat.
- **Red Thread Bracelet** – Fuels energy.
- **Hand on Heart Ritual** – Anchor words in chest.
- **Mirror Practice Spell** – Rehearse before mirror.
- **Copper Coin in Pocket** – Aids eloquence.
- **Bell Ring Before Speech** – Calls attention.
- **Honey Drop Ritual** – Taste honey for sweet words.
- **Hand Symbol Drawing** – Draw sigil on palm.
- **Sandalwood Smoke** – Calm nerves, focus.
- **Warm Water Sip** – Soothes voice.

CHARMS FOR STRENGTH IN CONFLICT

- **Iron Key Pocket** – Symbol of strength.

- **Garlic Clove Carry** – Repels intimidation.
- **Nail Cross Charm** – Iron nails crossed in pouch.
- **Circle Stance Ritual** – Stand with feet wide.
- **Peppercorn in Pocket** – Boldness booster.
- **Chant: "I Am Here"** – Repeat three times.
- **Clenched Fist Ritual** – Squeeze tight, release slowly.
- **Shoe Stamp Charm** – Stamp ground to claim space.
- **Cold Water Splash** – Resets anger.
- **Red Candle Burn** – Fuels courage.

Charms for Ambition & Long-Term Power

- **Planting Ritual** – Grow plant for self-confidence.
- **Knotting Cord with Goals** – Tie knots, bind success.
- **Morning Sun Ritual** – Face sunrise daily.
- **Mirror Covered at Night** – Rest without judgment.
- **Salt Jar on Desk** – Absorbs doubt.
- **Bread Slice Bite Before Work** – Grounds power.
- **Gold Object Carry** – Shiny attracts authority.
- **Pen with Ribbon Charm** – For ambitious writing.
- **Circle Drawing Ritual** – Draw circle around goals.
- **Lantern Lighting** – Night ritual for inner light.

Charms for Recovering Confidence

- **Bath with Rose Petals** – Restores dignity.
- **Clothes Brushing Ritual** – Brush clothes before going out.
- **Salt Toss Over Shoulder** – Casts off self-doubt.
- **Chalk Word Ritual** – Write bold word in chalk.
- **Apple Bite Charm** – Symbol of daring.
- **Drum Beat Meditation** – Beat steady rhythm.
- **Dance Alone** – Physical reclaiming of energy.
- **Fireplace Staring** – Gaze at fire for courage.
- **Mirror Bow Ritual** – Bow to self, honor strength

APPENDIX T:
CHARMS FOR PEACEFUL ENDINGS AND LETTING GO

CHARMS FOR ENDING RELATIONSHIPS

- **Ribbon Cutting Ritual** – Cut tied ribbon.
- **Candle Burn-Out** – Let candle burn fully.
- **Paper Writing Release** – Write name, burn paper.
- **Stone Toss in River** – Cast stone with intention.
- **Bread Crust Burying** – Bury crust to end bond.
- **Salt Line Break** – Sweep salt line outdoors.
- **Flower Petal Scattering** – Scatter petals, walk away.
- **Knotted Thread Unraveling** – Untie knot slowly.
- **Mirror Face Away** – Turn mirror from self.
- **Bell Toll Ritual** – Ring bell once, close chapter.

CHARMS FOR ENDING HABITS

- **Paper Knot Charm** – Tie knot, burn paper.
- **Glass of Water Ritual** – Drink water, pour rest away.
- **Candle Snuff** – Snuff candle with fingers.
- **Stone in Pocket** – Carry stone, discard at end.
- **Bread Slice Ritual** – Eat half, throw half away.
- **Salt Bath Cleansing** – Wash off habit.
- **Garlic Peel Charm** – Peel garlic clove, discard peel.
- **Thread Burn** – Burn thread tied around wrist.
- **Mirror Statement** – Say aloud: *"This ends."*
- **Hand Wash Ritual** – Wash hands firmly.

CHARMS FOR GRIEF & MOURNING

- **Black Candle Ritual** – Burn candle for mourning.
- **Stone Altar** – Build stone cairn outdoors.

- **Saltwater Bowl** – Symbol of tears.
- **Bread Offering** – Leave bread outdoors.
- **Bell Ring at Dusk** – Toll for remembrance.
- **White Flower Vase** – Place white blooms.
- **Mirror Covering** – Cover mirrors in grief.
- **Photo with Candle** – Burn candle near image.
- **Water Pouring Ritual** – Pour water in earth.
- **Chalk Word Memorial** – Write name in chalk.

CHARMS FOR JOBS OR PROJECTS ENDING

- **Box Packing Ritual** – Pack with calmness.
- **Ribbon Tie Bundle** – Bundle papers, tie ribbon.
- **Candle Burn-Down** – Candle marks closure.
- **Salt Sprinkle at Door** – Leave clean space.
- **Bread Sharing Goodbye** – Share food at farewell.
- **Bell Ring in Room** – Close space with sound.
- **Mirror Facing Outward** – Reflects past away.
- **Lantern Extinguish Ritual** – Blow lantern flame.
- **Chalk Circle Erasing** – Erase chalk circle.
- **Key Return Ritual** – Hand over key mindfully.

CHARMS FOR MOVING FORWARD

- **Planting New Seed** – Symbolizes new start.
- **Sunrise Watch** – Fresh day ritual.
- **Salt Line at Threshold** – Step over into future.
- **Coin Toss into Fountain** – Wish moving forward.
- **Hair Trim Ritual** – Cut lock of hair.
- **New Shoes First Step** – Symbol of onward journey.
- **Mirror Smile Ritual** – Smile at new reflection.
- **Bread Baking** – Nourishes future.
- **Lantern Lighting** – Guides new path.
- **Word Chant** – Speak new word aloud.

APPENDIX U
CHARMS FOR PROTECTION OF CHILDREN & FAMILY

CHARMS FOR INFANTS & CHILDREN

- **Salt in Pocket Hem** – Pinch of salt sewn into clothing hem.
- **Red Thread Bracelet** – Simple protection against envy.
- **Iron Pin in Blanket** – Pin discreetly near cradle edge.
- **Bell Charm on Door** – Tinkling warns of spirits.
- **Bread Crust Token** – Place under pillow for peaceful dreams.
- **Flower Water Sprinkle** – Rose water sprinkle over child.
- **Garlic Clove in Corner** – Repels malice.
- **Knot Charm on Cord** – Knot cord above cradle.
- **Silver Spoon Gift** – Symbol of protection.
- **Lantern by Cradle** – Flame near (but safe from) bed.

CHARMS FOR HOUSEHOLD UNITY

- **Salt Bowl on Table** – Shared safety.
- **Bread Loaf Blessing** – Family breaks bread together.
- **Ribbon Knot on Door** – Tie ribbon at entrance.
- **Iron Nail in Threshold** – Protective anchor.
- **Candle Circle at Dinner** – Light candles in circle.
- **Stone Cairn in Yard** – Family builds stone pile.
- **Photo Blessing Ritual** – Pass hand over family photo.
- **Handholding Circle** – Family circle with spoken word.
- **Chalk Heart on Doorstep** – Symbol of harmony.
- **Lantern Walk Together** – Night walk as bonding protection.

Charms Against Illness

- **Onion in Corner** – Draws away sickness.
- **Salt Jar in Room** – Absorbs heaviness.
- **Smoke Bath with Sage or Rosemary** – Clears air.
- **Bread Offering Outdoors** – Appeases wandering spirits.
- **Water Bowl by Bed** – Draws fever.
- **Egg Rolling Ritual** – Roll egg over child, discard.
- **Peppermint Steam Inhalation** – Clears breathing.
- **Chalk Sun on Wall** – Symbol of health.
- **Apple Slice Snack** – Strengthens vitality.
- **Daily Candle Blessing** – Burn white candle for health.

Charms for Safety at Night

31. **Lantern in Window** – Guides safety.
32. **Iron Object Under Bed** – Nail, key, or knife.
33. **Salt Line at Threshold** – Barrier against harm.
34. **Prayer at Doorway** – Spoken blessing.
35. **Bell Ring at Bedtime** – Clears energy.
36. **Knot Untying Ritual** – Untie knot to release worries.
37. **Mirror Turned Away** – Prevents disturbance.
38. **Bread Under Pillow** – Symbol of nourishment.
39. **Toy Blessing Ritual** – Bless toy with hand.
40. **Dream Chant** – Whisper protective phrase.

Charms for Protection on Journeys

- **Ribbon in Hair or Pocket** – For safe return.
- **Coin Kiss Ritual** – Child kisses coin, carries it.
- **Garlic in Bag** – Ward against harm.
- **Salt Pinch in Shoe** – Protection underfoot.
- **Stone Token Carry** – Each family member carries one.
- **Shared Meal Before Leaving** – Nourishment ensures connection.

- **Bell Ring Before Journey** – Bless departure.
- **Chalk Symbol on Door** – Family mark for return.
- **Candle Burned at Home** – Keeps connection alive.
- **Welcome Meal Ritual** – Food prepared for return.

Appendix V:
Charms for Household Harmony

Charms for a Peaceful Home

- **Salt at Doorways** – Prevents quarrels from entering.
- **Lantern by Window** – Warm welcome.
- **Bread on Table** – Symbol of nourishment.
- **Broom Behind Door** – Wards unwanted guests.
- **Bell at Entrance** – Harmony greeting.
- **Garlic Braid in Kitchen** – Safety charm.
- **Photo with Candle Ritual** – Family image blessed with flame.
- **Flower Vase on Table** – Freshens bonds.
- **Hand Clap Ritual** – Breaks tension.
- **Circle of Chairs** – Equality in conversation.

Charms for Banishing Quarrels

- **Salt Toss in Corner** – Clears lingering anger.
- **Bread Slice Sharing** – Share bread after argument.
- **Ribbon Cutting Ceremony** – Symbol of cutting discord.
- **Stone Toss Outdoors** – Throw quarrel away.
- **Candle Snuff Together** – Close conflict.
- **Bell Ring in Room** – Reset space.
- **Garlic Burn Ritual** – Smoke drives away tension.
- **Mirror Covering** – Rest after fight.
- **Joint Meal of Sweet Foods** – Heal with honey.
- **Plant Watering Ritual** – Nurture new peace.

Charms for Welcoming Guests

- **Salt Bowl Offering** – Place salt in visible bowl.
- **Bread & Salt Gift** – Traditional blessing.

- **Lantern Lit at Arrival** – Guests feel safe.
- **Bell Ring at Threshold** – Invites harmony.
- **Flower Gift to Guest** – Natural blessing.
- **Chair Circle Arrangement** – No hierarchy.
- **Sweet Drink Offering** – Mead, tea, or juice.
- **Hand Wash Ritual** – Offer water to cleanse.
- **Joint Candle Lighting** – Shared flame.
- **Thanksgiving Phrase** – Spoken words of welcome.

CHARMS FOR HEARTH & KITCHEN

- **Bread Baking on Sunday** – Weekly grounding.
- **Salt Jar on Shelf** – Absorbs quarrels.
- **Bell in Kitchen** – Rings before meals.
- **Garlic or Onion Hanging** – Household shield.
- **Wooden Spoon Blessing** – Bless cooking spoon.
- **Pot Stirring Clockwise** – Symbol of harmony.
- **Lantern Lit During Meal** – Warmth shared.
- **Joint Meal Cooking** – Participation builds peace.
- **Apple Slices Shared** – Sweetness spread.
- **Table Knock Ritual** – Knock wood for luck.

CHARMS FOR HOUSEHOLD PROSPERITY & JOY

- **Coin at Hearth** – Prosperity charm.
- **Flower Planting at Doorstep** – Blooms invite joy.
- **Bell Above Fireplace** – Calls abundance.
- **Ribbon Woven Through Curtains** – Harmony in daily life.
- **Stone in Window Sill** – Strengthens home foundation.
- **Mirror Facing Inward** – Reflects joy back.
- **Saltwater Wash of Floors** – Cleansing.
- **Joint Song Ritual** – Singing together binds hearts.
- **Lantern at Dinner** – Joyful centerpiece.
- **Bread Offering Outdoors** – Share abundance.

APPENDIX W:
CHARMS FOR JUSTICE & FAIRNESS

Justice charms aim to balance the scales, reveal truth, and ensure fairness. Folk magic often framed justice as weighing, cutting, or binding — sympathetic acts that mirrored court decisions, truth-finding, or redressing wrongs.

CHARMS FOR REVEALING TRUTH

- **Mirror Facing Opponent** – Truth reflects back.
- **Salt Water Glass** – Truth rises clear in water.
- **Candle Flame Test** – Speak words; flame flicker = truth.
- **Feather on Hand Ritual** – Lightness aligns with honesty.
- **Egg in Bowl of Water** – Cracks reveal hidden things.
- **Silver Coin on Paper** – Truth attracted to purity.
- **Bell Ring Questioning** – Ring once after each claim.
- **Mirror Writing Ritual** – Write backward; hidden truth revealed.
- **Circle Drawing Interrogation** – Sit inside circle for fairness.
- **Iron Nail Pointing** – Nail directs to truth.

CHARMS FOR LEGAL MATTERS

- **Salt in Pocket at Court** – Protection charm.
- **Iron Key in Hand** – Unlocks fair outcome.
- **Bay Leaf Under Tongue** – Eloquence in speech.
- **Ribbon Knot in Pocket** – Holds judge's favor.
- **Paper with Scales Drawing** – Balance symbol.
- **Coin Offering Before Hearing** – Appeases fate.
- **Bell Ring at Dawn** – Calls justice.
- **Black & White Candle Burn** – Balance of opposites.
- **Chalk Line Ritual** – Draw straight line, walk it.
- **Stone in Shoe** – Reminder to stand firm.

- **Write your case number** - put it on scale with the other side having equal weight papers on it saying 'truth' and 'Justice'

CHARMS FOR FAIRNESS IN COMMUNITY

- **Circle Dance** – Equality in movement.
- **Bread Sharing** – Each receives portion.
- **Lantern in Center** – Shared light.
- **Bell Ring in Square** – Calls balance.
- **Saltwater Sprinkle** – Neutralizes quarrels.
- **Chalk Circle Discussion** – Everyone equal.
- **Ribbon Knot Exchange** – Binding fairness.
- **Coin Toss Ritual** – Decision by chance.
- **Stone Cairn Building** – Symbol of balance.
- **Song Singing Together** – Collective voice.

CHARMS FOR REDRESSING WRONGS

- **Paper Burn Ritual** – Burn injustice written down.
- **Feather Toss in Wind** – Release grievances.
- **Stone Toss in River** – Cast wrongs away.
- **Salt Rub on Hands** – Clean injustice.
- **Candle Snuff** – End cycle of unfairness.
- **Ribbon Cutting** – Sever wrong ties.
- **Mirror Turned Away** – End reflection of injustice.
- **Bread Offering Outdoors** – Appease spirits of balance.
- **Bell Toll at Sunset** – Close quarrel.
- **Planting New Tree** – Begin fresh fairness.

CHARMS FOR PERSONAL JUSTICE

- **Hand on Heart Chant** – *"Balance flows through me."*
- **Stone Carry Charm** – Symbol of steadfastness.
- **Salt Bath Ritual** – Wash away imbalance.

- **Feather in Hat** – Honor personal dignity.
- **Lantern Walk Alone** – Walk by lantern light, clarity.
- **Bread Crust Under Pillow** – Dream guidance.
- **Iron Spoon in Kitchen** – Steadfastness.
- **Candle Gaze Meditation** – Center self.
- **Coin Gift to Stranger** – Fairness given outward.
- **Bell Ring Alone** – Affirmation of truth.

Appendix X: Charms for Memory & Wisdom

Charms for Memory in Study

- **Bay Leaf Under Pillow** – Retains knowledge.
- **Peppermint Chew** – Clears thoughts.
- **Book Knot Charm** – Tie thread in book.
- **Apple Bite While Reading** – Sharpens focus.
- **Candlelight Reading** – Sacred illumination.
- **Salt Packet in Pocket** – Grounds attention.
- **Copper Coin Carry** – Symbol of clarity.
- **Thread Bookmark** – Memory anchored.
- **Stone Token on Desk** – Focus point.
- **Mirror Glance Before Exam** – Call back learning.

Charms for Long-Term Wisdom

- **Oak Leaf Carry** – Tree of wisdom.
- **Saltwater Rinse** – Clears old thoughts.
- **Feather in Hat** – Sign of learning.
- **Bell Ring Each Morning** – Awakens clarity.
- **Candle on Book Ritual** – Burn flame while studying.
- **Honey Drop Ritual** – Sweetens knowledge.
- **Circle Drawing** – Symbol of wholeness.
- **Stone Pile Building** – Patience ritual.
- **Lantern Walk at Dusk** – Reflective wisdom.
- **Mirror Meditation** – Wisdom reflected inward.

Charms for Recalling Dreams

- **Notebook by Bed** – Record dreams.
- **Bay Leaf Under Pillow** – Enhances recall.
- **Salt Line on Headboard** – Seals dream space.

- **Candle Snuff Before Sleep** – Clears mind.
- **Apple Slice Night Ritual** – Sweetens dream memory.
- **Stone Under Pillow** – Anchors dreams.
- **Feather Above Bed** – Dream catcher symbol.
- **Thread Bracelet** – Binds dreams to self.
- **Water Glass at Bedside** – Absorbs dream confusion.
- **Mirror Covered** – Keeps dreams intact.

CHARMS FOR ELDERS' WISDOM

- **Lantern Lighting at Sunset** – Honors elders.
- **Bread Baking Together** – Knowledge passed.
- **Salt Gift** – Symbol of wisdom.
- **Photo Blessing** – Ancestors remembered.
- **Stone Cairn Ritual** – Layered memory.
- **Feather Writing** – Write with quill, wisdom flows.
- **Circle of Chairs** – Elders at center.
- **Bell Ring for Ancestors** – Summons wisdom.
- **Garlic Offering Outdoors** – Strength and memory.
- **Mirror Storytelling Ritual** – Tell stories before mirror.

CHARMS FOR ONGOING CLARITY

- **Morning Water Drink** – Clears mind.
- **Salt Bath Reset** – Memory cleansing.
- **Knot Untying Ritual** – Loosens confusion.
- **Stone Carry Token** – Steadiness.
- **Lantern Lit During Work** – Guidance.
- **Apple Bite Each Morning** – Fresh wisdom.
- **Peppermint Tea Ritual** – Mental sharpness.
- **Bell Toll at Noon** – Midday clarity.
- **Bread Slice Offering** – Nourishment of thought.
- **Mirror Smile Ritual** – Self-trust in wisdom.

APPENDIX Y
CHARMS FOR SAFE JOURNEYS ABROAD

Travel magic is ancient. When leaving home, protection focuses on thresholds, offerings, and guiding symbols. Abroad, charms often involve coins, shoes, food, and stars.

CHARMS BEFORE DEPARTURE

- **Bread Slice Shared** – Family meal.
- **Salt Pinch in Shoe** – Protection on path.
- **Coin Gift to Traveler** – Luck token.
- **Ribbon Knot in Luggage** – Tied safety.
- **Lantern Lit at Departure** – Guides traveler.
- **Bell Ring Before Leaving** – Blesses path.
- **Hand on Doorframe Ritual** – Leave blessing.
- **Chalk Symbol on Doorstep** – Travel mark.
- **Mirror Covered Until Return** – Holds presence.
- **Plant Watering Ritual** – Symbol of safe return.
- **Put a four leaf clover by your passport** - for luck

CHARMS DURING TRAVEL

- **Stone in Pocket** – Grounding.
- **Garlic in Bag** – Ward.
- **Salt Packet in Wallet** – Neutralizer.
- **Red Thread Bracelet** – Luck abroad.
- **Coin in Left Shoe** – Protects steps.
- **Feather in Book** – Travel token.
- **Lantern or Candle Image** – Carry picture of light
- **Bell Token Charm** – Sound guidance.
- **Bread Crust in Bag** – Nourishment.
- **Water Bottle Blessing** – Vitality.

Charms in Foreign Lands

- **Coin Offering at Shrine** – Respect spirits.
- **Bread Gift to Stranger** – Build goodwill.
- **Lantern Lit in Room** – Mark safe space.
- **Salt Sprinkle at Threshold** – Claim lodging.
- **Mirror Facing Out** – Protects from spirits.
- **Bell Ring in Room** – Clear air.
- **Chalk Symbol on Luggage** – Prevent loss.
- **Stone from Home Carried** – Anchor spirit.
- **Thread Knot Bracelet** – Binds safe return.
- **Garlic Clove in Window** – Guard room.

Charms for Return Home

- **Coin Toss in Water Abroad** – Ensures return.
- **Ribbon Cut at Homecoming** – Release travel spell.
- **Lantern Lit at Home** – Welcomes back.
- **Salt Bath Ritual** – Cleanse travel dust.
- **Bread Sharing Again** – Celebrate safe return.
- **Bell Ring at Doorway** – Announce arrival.
- **Mirror Uncovered** – Rejoin home.
- **Stone Returned Outdoors** – Replace stone carried.
- **Thanksgiving Offering Outdoors** – Gratitude.
- **Plant Watering on Return** – Symbol of continuity.

Charms for Long-Term Travelers

- **Photo Blessing Ritual** – Carry loved ones' photo.
- **Letter Writing Charm** – Anchor to home.
- **Salt Packet Exchanged** – Family shares salt.
- **Ribbon Cut in Two** – One piece carried.
- **Bread Starter Shared** – Family bond.
- **Lantern Kept Burning at Home** – Vigil.

- **Bell Tolls Weekly** – Reminder of connection.
- **Stone Under Pillow While Away** – Comfort.
- **Chalk Circle Ritual** – Anchor when lonely.
- **Mirror Gaze Before Leaving Each Place** – Ground self.

APPENDIX Z:
CHARMS FOR WEATHER & NATURE

Weather charms harness sympathetic action: water for rain, fire for sun, noise for storms, stillness for calm. Farmers and wanderers relied on such practices.

CHARMS FOR RAIN CALLING

- **Water Pouring Outdoors** – Symbolic rain.
- **Bowl Left in Yard** – Invite clouds.
- **Leaf Sprinkling Ritual** – Shake leaves dipped in water.
- **Song of Rain** – Chant rhythmic.
- **Drum Beat Ritual** – Mimic thunder.
- **Stone Toss in Water** – Summon ripples.
- **Lantern Extinguish Outdoors** – Call clouds.
- **Clothing Hung Outdoors** – Invite rain.
- **Bell Ring to Sky** – Call attention.
- **Salt Dissolved in Water** – Sky receives.
- **Go outside with an umbrella and wellies on**

CHARMS FOR SUNLIGHT

- **Candle Lighting Outdoors** – Symbol of sun.
- **Mirror Facing Sky** – Reflects sun.
- **Golden Cloth on Ground** – Invite warmth.
- **Apple Offering** – Fruit of sun.
- **Bell Ring at Noon** – Solar time.
- **Lantern Lit with Gold Paper** – Attracts light.
- **Bread Slice Outdoors** – Nourishment for sun.
- **Feather Raised Skyward** – Air meets fire.
- **Chalk Sun Symbol** – Drawn on ground.
- **Stone Circle Ritual** – Align with sun.
- **Put suncream on** - setting an intent

Charms Against Storms

- **Iron Nail in Ground** – Anchors home.
- **Salt Line at Doorway** – Barrier.
- **Lantern Lit Inside** – Household courage.
- **Bell Ring in Storm** – Breaks fear.
- **Prayer Chanted Together** – Collective calm.
- **Mirror Covered Indoors** – Avoid lightning attraction.
- **Broom Laid Across Door** – Traditional storm block.
- **Bread Offering Outdoors** – Appease winds.
- **Feather Weight Ritual** – Hold feather, calm winds.
- **Stone Cairn by House** – Anchor energy.

Charms for Seasonal Balance

- **Planting Seed at Equinox** – Renewal.
- **Lantern Lighting at Solstice** – Light return.
- **Salt Jar Changed Quarterly** – Seasonal reset.
- **Bread Sharing at Festivals** – Community harmony.
- **Bell Ring at Dawn & Dusk** – Balance cycles.
- **Circle Dance Outdoors** – Seasonal flow.
- **Stone Stacking Ritual** – Balance nature.
- **Mirror Facing Sky on Equinox** – Reflect balance.
- **Candle Burn at Solstice Night** – Endurance.
- **Water Pouring at Summer Heat** – Balance fire.

Charms for Nature Connection

- **Tree Hug Ritual** – Direct bond.
- **Stone Carry from River** – Grounding.
- **Feather Collection** – Air wisdom.
- **Salt Sprinkle on Soil** – Blessing.
- **Bread Offering to Birds** – Sharing abundance.
- **Lantern Hung in Tree** – Tree spirit offering.
- **Bell Ring at Forest Edge** – Call guardians.

- **Circle Walk Outdoors** – Align with earth.
- **Chalk Symbol on Rock** – Mark presence.
- **Water Sip Outdoors** – Honor cycles.

Glossary

This glossary provides definitions and explanations of key terms, concepts, and symbols used throughout the book. It's designed to help readers deepen their understanding of sympathetic magic and its practices.

Altar: A dedicated space for rituals, often holding symbolic objects like candles, stones, or herbs.
Amulet: An object charged with protective or magical energy, often carried or worn.
Banishing: A ritual or charm designed to remove negativity, obstacles, or unwanted energy.
Binding: A practice that symbolically ties or secures energy, often used for protection or commitment.
Charm: A small ritual or object imbued with intention, used to attract or repel specific energies.
Cleansing: The act of purifying a space, object, or person of negative or stagnant energy.
Correspondences: The symbolic connections between objects, colors, elements, and intentions (e.g., red for passion, coins for prosperity).
Divination: The practice of seeking insight or guidance through symbolic tools like tarot cards, runes, or candle flames.
Elements: The four classical elements—Earth, Air, Fire, Water—often used in rituals to represent different energies.
Evil Eye: A belief in a harmful gaze or curse, often countered with protective charms.
Folk Magic: Traditional, often practical, magic passed down through generations, rooted in cultural practices.
Grimoire: A book of magical knowledge, spells, and rituals.
Hoodoo: A folk magic tradition rooted in African American culture, often incorporating herbs, roots, and symbolic objects.
Herbalism: The use of plants and herbs for their magical, medicinal, or symbolic properties.
Intention: The focused thought or purpose behind a ritual or charm, considered the driving force of magic.

Knot Magic: The use of knots in cords or ribbons to bind, release, or channel energy.
Mojo Bag: A small pouch filled with symbolic objects (herbs, stones, etc.) used to attract or repel specific energies.
Moon Phases: The cycles of the moon (New, Waxing, Full, Waning) often used to time rituals for specific purposes.
Prosperity Magic: Practices designed to attract abundance, wealth, and opportunity.
Protection Magic: Charms or rituals used to shield against harm, negativity, or unwanted influences.
Ritual: A structured practice or ceremony performed with intention, often involving symbolic actions or objects.
Sigil: A symbolic design or mark created to represent a specific intention or desire.
Sympathetic Magic: The principle that like attracts like, and that objects or actions can influence reality through symbolic connection.
Talisman: An object charged with specific energy, often used to attract or amplify desired outcomes.
Warding: Practices used to protect a space or person from negative energies or influences.
Zodiac: The astrological system of signs and symbols, often used to align rituals with cosmic energies.

www.ingramcontent.com/pod-product-compliance
Lightning Source LLC
Chambersburg PA
CBHW022216090526
44584CB00012BB/672